Making Stop Motion Films

Anne Ploegman

Making Stop Motion Films

Copyright © 2020 Anne Ploegman

All rights reserved.

No part of this book may be reproduced in any form without written permission from the copyright owner, except in the case of brief quotations in a book review.

ISBN: 9798615094125

All photography copyright © 2020 Anne Ploegman, except:
Susan Ploegman, photo of author back cover.

CONTENTS

INTRODUCTION	5
THE BASICS	6
MATERIALS, TOOLS, AND EQUIPMENT	8
BASIC TERMS AND THINGS TO KNOW	10
PREPRODUCTION	15
GENRES	16
FILM STYLES	18
WRITING THE STORY	19
BUDGETING A SHORT FILM	36
SETS, PUPPETS, AND PROPS INTRODUCTION	38
MAKING THE PUPPET	46
SET BUILDING	60
CREATING PROPS AND DECORATING	78
SCHEDULING THE FILM	95
PRODUCTION	98
EQUIPMENT AND TOOLS OVERVIEW	99
SETTING UP AND GETTING STARTED	103
STARTING TO ANIMATE	106
THE PUPPET'S MOVEMENT AND EFFECTS	116
WRAPPING THINGS UP	132
POSTPRODUCTION	**134**
EDITING	135
RECORDING VOICES AND SOUNDS	139
MUSIC	145
LIGHTING AND COLOUR	148
VISUAL EFFECTS	150
CREDITS	152
FINISHING UP	154
GETTING YOUR FILM OUT THERE	157

EXTRAS 165

    CREATING YOUR OWN STUDIO   165

    HOW TO MAKE PRINTABLES   167

    3 INGREDIENT CLAY RECIPE   170

    SUPER BASIC, QUICK SEWING GUIDE   171

INTRODUCTION

After creating many of my own stop motion videos and short films, using various experimenting and techniques, I decided to create a book about this process and help others see a real life example of how kids can make their own stop motion animated movies at home!

This book covers the process of planning for a film, writing scripts, making puppets, creating props, building sets, animating, recording sounds and voices, editing, and giving your film an audience. I have included many examples from my projects, including rough draft scripts, sketches, set building, and more. Along the way, you will pick up useful information and helpful tips to create your very own stop motion animations.

Keeping this book budget friendly, I show ways that I have created very low budget short films, using basic materials. This book is for those that have little or no experience with stop motion or for those who have been doing it for a while and need some extra helpful tips and practical ways to expand.

All you really need is a camera, phone or tablet, plus a computer, a few found materials, and the tools found in this book to get started! Stop motion animation is a very fun and creative activity, and I hope you enjoy the process!

Making Stop Motion Films

THE BASICS
WHAT DO I NEED TO START?

Before getting started with your movie, it is important to have an idea of what will be needed or used during the process. There are several types of tools out there for making films and videos, but I will be describing what I mainly use and find most practical.

While many professionals and some student filmmakers use expensive equipment to create their films, I try to work with what I have at home, first. If you can do that, eventually you will increase the items in your equipment collection over the years. I use my iPad mini for several things including filming, animating stop motions, and some editing. Although a professional camera would definitely give any short film a more polished and crisp look, right now I work with what I have to produce the best films I can. On the next page are the basic things I usually have at hand to create my own stop motion animations, but feel free to use whatever works best along the way.

MATERIALS, TOOLS, AND EQUIPMENT

MATERIALS

- Paper (recycled, scrapbook paper, printer paper, scraps, etc.)
- Glue (glue sticks, hot glue sticks, and clear-drying glue)
- Acrylic and watercolour paints
- Thread
- Fabric and felt
- Recycled cardboard
- Recycled paperboard (the thin cardboard material from pasta, cracker, or cereal boxes)
- Ribbon
- Wire
- Natural drying clay
- Buttons and beads
- Wooden craft sticks (craft sticks, dowels, skewers, etc.)
- Yarn
- Sticky tack (the blue blob in the first picture)
- Tape (a kind that won't remove paint from walls)

Many of these items can be found at local craft stores or dollar stores, but they also can be found around the house!

Making Stop Motion Films

TOOLS

- Ruler
- Paintbrushes
- Hot glue gun
- Sewing needles
- Knitting needles (optional)
- Crochet hooks (optional)
- Craft scissors
- Sewing scissors
- Pliers
- Utility knife
- Old pruners (for cutting craft sticks)
- Painting palette
- Pen and pencil

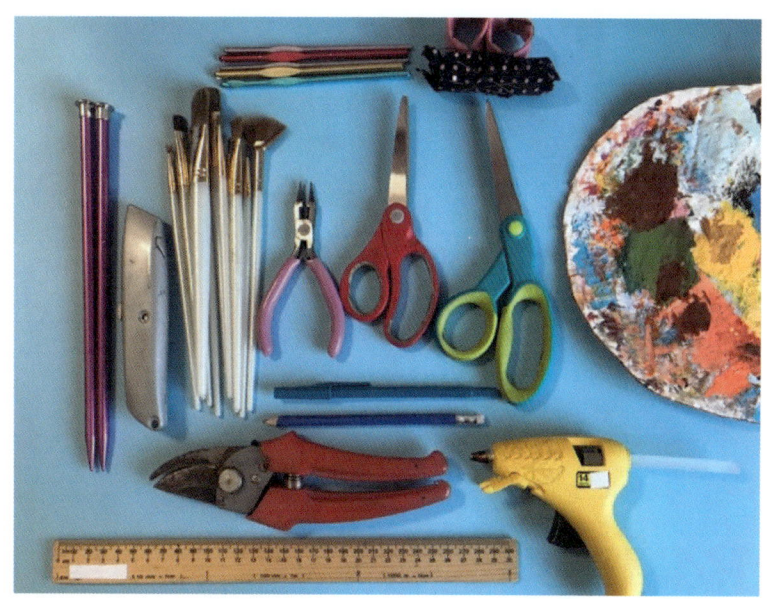

WARNING: Some of the tools listed could be dangerous and require extreme caution. Make sure to ask an adult for help or supervision when using anything hot or sharp.

EQUIPMENT AND SOFTWARE/APPS

- Camera (or use a phone, tablet, etc.)
- Tripod (or other methods of support for the camera)
- Computer
- Editing software
- Stop motion app or software

More details on equipment will be covered later in this book.

BASIC TERMS AND THINGS TO KNOW

Here I will be covering some common term meanings and helpful things to know before beginning.

WHAT IS STOP MOTION?

A stop motion animation is made up of a series of photographs, with the objects being slightly moved each time, to create the illusion of movement. Basically, stop motion is an animation technique created using physical items including puppets, sets, and props. Each time, the puppet or item is slightly moved and photographed, until there are enough frames (pictures) to create the movement. If you want your character to wave their hand, you would need to take a picture of the character, move their hand very slightly, take a picture, and then repeat until the character has accomplished the movement. Essentially, the less you move your character each time, and the more pictures taken, each slightly different from the last, the smoother your animation will be.

WHAT ARE SOME STOP MOTION MOVIES?

- *Frankenweenie*
- *Kubo and the Two Strings*
- *Fantastic Mr. Fox*
- *The Boxtrolls*

WHAT IS CLAYMATION?

Claymation is a method of animation that involves clay figures being moved and photographed. It is the same as stop motion animation, but it is being made using puppets that are sculpted from non-drying modelling clay.

WHAT ARE SOME CLAYMATION MOVIES?

- *Chicken Run*
- *Wallace & Gromit: The Curse of the Were-Rabbit*
- *Shaun the Sheep Movie*
- *Early Man*

I mostly work with non-clay puppets when I make my stop motion films. As I am not as experienced with working and sculpting clay puppets for stop motion, I will not be showing as many claymation examples here. If you are interested in claymation, I recommend using the techniques and ideas in this book, which can be applied to any form of stop motion.

WHAT DOES FPS MEAN?

Fps is the abbreviation for **frames per second**. A frame is a single picture. Fps means the frame rate and the amount of still images that are going to be played for every second of your film. If your film is set to 10 fps, it means 10 photos will be shown for every second. In other words, 10 photos will be one second of the video. The higher fps your film is set to the smoother it will appear, but it also means you must take more pictures.

Professional stop motion animators do about 24 fps, which is very time consuming and can take years to complete as a full length film.

HOW MANY FPS SHOULD I DO?

If you are using a stop motion app or software (I will get into this later) you can adjust the amount of fps in the settings. When I started out, I did around 6 fps and currently do 15 fps. I think this is a good speed as the animation is smooth looking, but it is not as time consuming as 24 fps. If you are just starting out, I recommend around 6-10 fps. You may want to experiment with what works best. Remember, less fps may take less time to animate, but it also looks choppier. It is okay for just beginning since as you progress you will eventually get used to a higher setting.

WHAT DOES CGI AND VFX MEAN?

CGI is the abbreviation for **computer generated imagery**. It means the images and animation are created on a computer software, rather than physically, like stop motion. Many movies are completely animated using CGI. Stop motion animation is not CGI, although CGI and stop motion can be combined to create different effects.

VFX means **visual effects**. Many movies use computer generated VFX to create different special effects in the scene.

When starting out, special effects created on the computer are not necessary. I generally do not use many or any computer generated imagery or effects. I prefer and enjoy creating most things physically and I will be showing ways I do this.

WHAT IS GREEN/BLUE SCREEN?

You probably have heard of green or blue screen technology, which basically is done with a bright green or blue backdrop that is later changed on the computer to become any scene or background imaginable. All that is needed is a bright green or blue background to place behind your characters. Then using editing software, you can change the image. You just have to make sure nothing else except the background is green or blue, otherwise those objects will change into the new background, too. I used to work with green screen a lot, but I also liked how creative I could get with my own hand painted backgrounds and handmade sets. Green screen can also be an exciting way to add fun backgrounds to a scene and try out different effects.

HOW LONG DOES A STOP MOTION FILM TAKE TO ANIMATE?

It really depends on a number of things: how long the film is, the number of fps, the complexity of the movement, and the overall film itself. I used to create a stop motion video of around 1.5-4 minutes long, almost every week for my YouTube channel. It usually took around 4-7 hours to animate. I took a couple breaks, but mostly was doing hours of constant animating. My short films are around 2-8 minutes long, so I take much more time on them than I did with my YouTube videos. I also want my short films to be as good as they can be, so I take my time. Overall, my short films take about 10-30 hours to animate, but the preparation beforehand can take over 100 hours, if the film is made by scratch.

WHAT IS A SHORT FILM?

A short film does not really have a specific length requirement. It is any film that tells a story from beginning to end, and it could even be as short as about 1 minute. Film festivals (I will talk about film festivals later) have their own rules for what qualifies as a short film, which I have found is usually around 15 minutes and under. Some are shorter and some are longer. Short films tell stories in unique points of view and are great for students while full length films are much more time consuming.

PREPRODUCTION
BRAINSTORMING IDEAS AND INSPIRATION

Now we have reached a stage in filmmaking called **preproduction**. Preproduction begins with brainstorming a film, and ends right before the beginning of animating, which is called **production**. Everything after a film has finished being animated (or filmed) is called **postproduction**, which is when I do recording and editing.

When working in preproduction, I will brainstorm my film, get ideas, draw pictures, and write about my future characters. I also think about the style and genre of my film, what materials I want my puppets to be made of, etc. Then, still in preproduction, I write the script, draw a storyboard, and make all the puppets, props and sets. It is a lot of work. My last preproduction lasted over 100 hours. It does not always take that long, as I used to make a stop motion video almost every week using my toys and dolls.

Planning is very important and will save you from some mistakes or work when you are animating. When I made a lot of stop motion videos with my toys, I did not do very much planning. I often didn't even write a script or an outline of my film. I just thought of an idea, and then I made the video. This is okay for videos when you are just beginning or just want to jump in and make something quick and fun. If you are thinking about making something more complex, detailed or long, a lot of planning is essential and extremely helpful.

GENRES

Before I begin writing the story for my film, as I am writing it, or sometimes after the story is written, I think about or determine what genre it is/will be. Genre means the category that your film is in. There are several genres: comedy, action, adventure, science fiction, fantasy, and more. Any unspecified film that cannot be categorized into a specific genre is an experimental film. Genres can be combined or include elements from other genres. I like making comedies, with a few elements from other genres such as fantasy. The important thing about your film is that there is a balance.

Here are just a few genres, based on the family/kids movies I have seen:

COMEDY

A comedy is a movie that is supposed to be funny and make the audience laugh.

ACTION

Action films usually have more action scenes than talking ones. Some examples include superhero or secret agent movies.

ADVENTURE

An adventure film may include some sort of exploration, discovery, or adventure through something such as a jungle, new universe, or maybe a fairytale world.

SCIENCE FICTION

Science fiction is a genre that includes anything fictional that could exist because of science.

FANTASY

Unlike science fiction, fantasy films are movies with magical worlds and creatures that never could exist. Fantasy films usually use magic as its explanation, rather than science, which separates the two genres.

Think about your genre as you go along with your brainstorming, planning, and writing.

FILM STYLES

Every film should have a developed and unique style that will give it a distinctive appearance. That includes everything from its colour palette to its costumes. When making a film, you should stick to a certain style to avoid things from looking unorganized or confusing. The style can be from any genre, and has a lot to do with the time frame, characters, and story. For example, a fantasy film set in a time of the past may look vintage, whimsical, and colourful. Creating an inspiration board or collection of items, such as paint chips or cut-outs from magazines, can help develop your film's style, colour palette, and theme.

When I had a YouTube channel, the style of my stop motion videos was usually bright, modern, and fun. I made miniature doll rooms with popular décor, focusing on current trends to achieve this look. Now, I make my own puppets and dolls from scratch, and I am not always trying to achieve this look. I sometimes try to make my puppets vintage or old-fashioned looking. My short film, *Nursery Crimes* is very colourful and unique, but it is still vintage feeling. Now, I am currently working on a stop motion series that is colourful and playful. I am trying to make the style appear more fun and cheerful. It could be achieved by the way I make my puppets, design my sets, write my script, or paint backdrops. Eventually, with a lot of experimenting and deciding on what you like best, your style will naturally develop. I do not have the same style for everything I do; I like experimenting and trying different things.

WRITING THE STORY

Before I write the script for my film, I write about the story. Sometimes it is like a mini-book of the film, or other times it is just an outline or plot. It explains what happens in the beginning, middle, and end of the movie. I usually will change the story as I go along, but it is important to have an idea of what is going to happen before making sets, props, and puppets, even if the script is not completely finished. Sometimes I may write a few paragraphs of my short film, then I will develop my story further, adding in other elements, characters, problems, and solutions.

It is important to write using real life experiences. These are the most believable stories—ones that you have experienced in real life. It does not mean your stories cannot be unique, original, or fantastical; it just means there should be elements or characters in it that relate to your experiences and represent what you know.

IDEAS: WHERE DO THEY COME FROM?

All filmmakers get inspiration and ideas from other films, real life, and everything around them. I enjoy making films more than watching them, but watching is still important and necessary. Studying a film is different from just watching it. You do not always have to get out a piece of paper and take notes. I just watch a movie, and listen to the music, sounds, look at the different costumes, lighting and colour, and how it affects the story. I also pay close attention to the actors and how other viewers and I respond to the overall film.

Besides other movies, I get my ideas from real life. It could be a story I heard, an existing classic story that I want to change up, or ideas from real life experiences. Whenever I get a good idea, I write it down into my film notebook.

FILM NOTEBOOK AND SKETCHBOOK

I keep a large notebook dedicated to film. I write down everything from scripts, characters, sets, and prop ideas. I also have a sketchbook that is often used for illustrating my puppets that I want to make. When brainstorming a new short film, I write down an idea of the genre, style, colour palette, music, and characters I want. I also think about the setting, costumes, and props. Writing down a title before even making the script can help out a lot while developing the story. Some ideas can take months to develop, others are much quicker. If you keep a long list of ideas, eventually it will narrow down to a few ideas, which if still worthy, will become a film. Just keep trying things out and learning from mistakes. Some of my ideas are bad, but I keep thinking of new ones and trying until something works.

SHORT FILMS ARE UNIQUE

If you ever have seen an animated short film, you may have noticed that it probably would not work out as a full length film. Due to its length, a short film can be told in any unique way that may be a bit boring or strange as a full length film. I try to take advantage of this sometimes, but other times I want my short film to be more like a mini episode or movie.

FORMATTING AND WRITING THE SCREENPLAY

```
Scene 5
Int. Mrs. Bertie's Kitchen

                        (POV) JACKLYN
    Jacklyn follows Mrs. Bertie (who is stirring a pot) into her
                             kitchen.

                        Good afternoon.
    Mrs. Bertie's back is turned and she does not respond at first.

                          MRS. BERTIE

       (Grunts) I suppose you're here to snoop?

                         Turns around


                            JACKLYN

    (Laughs a little) I just wanted to know if Humpty was around
       your kitchen…yesterday. (Jacklyn stares at green footprints on
                  the ground and a black feather.)

                    (Background) MRS. BERTIE

      Well, I suppose, but it ain't any of your concern!


                    (Close on, black feather.)
                            JACKLYN

                     Well, um, thank you.

                          MRS. BERTIE

          (Extreme Close-up) (Suspicious) Hmmm.
```

When I am ready to write my script, I must make many decisions (not all at once). First, I need to make sure each scene will not be too long or too short. Second, I need to know how much dialogue (talking) there will be. Third, I need to make sure everything gets done in a reasonable amount of time—not too quickly or slowly. Actually, there are many more things I think about before writing the script. After deciding on a number of things, I will begin writing my first draft. On the previous page is an example of one of my scripts.

Before beginning, write the name of your film on the front page of your script. If you are still working on the name, that's okay. It will come to you as you go along or even when you finish the entire film.

Here are some of the things that need to be included in the script and film, and what they mean:

SETTING

The setting is where and when the action happens in the film. Think about what time the story takes place: past, present, or future? Where does the story take place at the beginning of the film and how does it change as the story moves on?

EXT. AND INT.

Ext. stands for *Exterior*, meaning scenes that are set outside.
Int. stands for *Interior*, meaning scenes that are set inside.

When writing a script, for each scene, I write down if the scene will be interior or exterior and where the scene actually takes place. I also may include the time of day and sometimes the weather, depending on how detailed I want to get.

There are a few different formatting rules that go along with writing a screenplay (I do not even use all of them), but as long as your screenplay is understandable and works for you and others who are working on the project, it is fine. In fact, a simple script may even work better for you or others to understand and make changes to it more easily.

All your script really needs is the title, scene, location, the action, and the lines for whoever is talking. Feel free to add in whatever you think will help you along the way.

HOW DOES THE STORY GO?

Although formatting a script in an organized way is useful, it will not make the script itself a good story. When I am writing the actual words and story for my screenplays, I take a number of things into account:

WHO IS TELLING THE STORY?

Is there an offscreen narrator telling the story? Is the narrator a character in the film? Who is the story unfolding through? From whose point of view is the story being told?

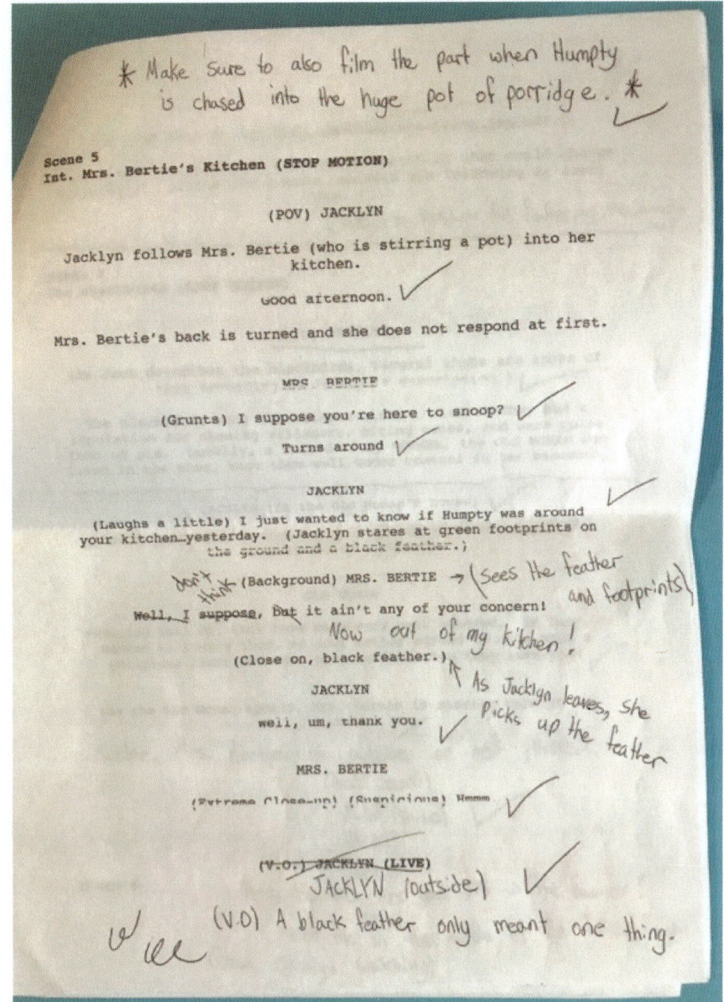

CHARACTER DEVELOPMENT: DO I KNOW MY CHARACTERS?

It is very important that you know and understand your characters. Before I start writing, I will draw many sketches of my characters and write about them. I will write about their strengths, weaknesses, fears, traits, interests, family history, etc. What are their qualities that especially stand out to the audience? I need to know my characters as if they were real people. This is challenging and sometimes very time consuming, but it really helps when deciding what the characters are going to say, do, or wear. What is my character's favourite colour? Least favourite? Does my character have any siblings? Where has my character lived in his/her life? What is my character afraid of? Do this before you begin writing: draw some pictures of your characters and create a mini biography of them. Include facts about them that may not even be part of the film. Adding in little extra background information is helpful when deciding on the bigger things the character will be doing.

The main character/protagonist should have a very developed personality, and he/she should be someone people would want to watch and connect with. The main character has to be relatable to your audience and feel like they could be a real, believable person.

CHARACTER PERSONALITY

I enjoy creating unique personalities for my characters. A lot of times, my characters have traits or behave in a way that is inspired by people I have seen or met in real life. Never give direct reference to a real life person without permission; instead, be inspired by them. I observe people, and I pay attention to their personality and how they act. I also think about how my character would act in certain situations. I will talk about making the characters' voices later on. For now, pay attention to people's tone of voice and how it matches their body language and gestures.

WHAT DOES THE MAIN CHARACTER /PROTAGONIST WANT?

In my films, I try to include something that the main character wants more than anything. It could be solving a mystery, becoming an astronaut, or winning a competition. It also could be a lot simpler than this. Throughout the film, I try to make it seem as if the main character will never get what they want. Although they try, there needs to be an obstacle in their way. In my film *Nursery Crimes*, my main character Jacklyn wants to solve the mystery above all else, but there also is a bit of a backstory included: she wants to prove her worthiness to her late father. Jacklyn feels guilty about letting her father down, and she needs to solve the greatest mystery, more than anything. At first things go smoothly, but one dark night she is greatly challenged.

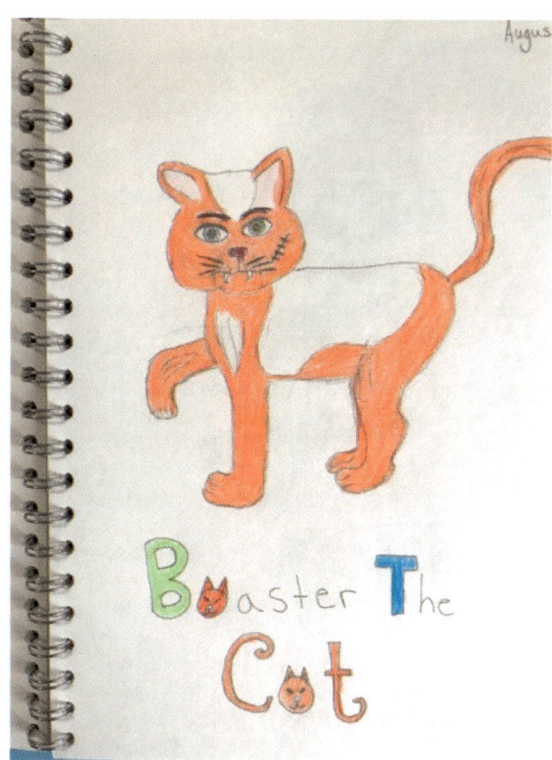

THE ANTAGONIST/CONFLICT:

In the script, there is some sort of conflict between the main character and somebody or something else. The problem could be something existing within the character's self, or it could be something within the character's environment. Here are some examples of conflicts: the protagonist is afraid of spiders and needs to overcome his/her fear, or the character has lost something very important. Of course, commonly, the issue is a villain. The villain may be an evil witch or a class bully. In many films (not always short films), there is not just one problem. That would be a bit boring. The problem needs to be more complicated, involving other people or things. Maybe the villain has a backstory relating to why he/she is causing trouble. I try to introduce the issue or villain near the beginning of my film, and I do not let things get solved too easily. In short films, I try to keep the problems minimal and basic, but I have imaginary problems with other characters, which helps determine their behaviour.

SOLVING THE PROBLEM IN THE FILM

As I mentioned earlier, I try to make the character struggle to get what they want or solve the problem in the story. The solution cannot just fall from the sky or unrealistically be solved just to conclude the story, unless you are going for something like that. The film should not be too predictable. Although with many films, it can be predicted that there will be a happy ending, but what led up to the ending is not always predictable.

Whatever happens throughout the film, there still needs to be an ending, which in many cases is a happy or at least a satisfying one, or maybe it's one that leaves the audience wondering what will happen next.

HOW DID THE MAIN CHARACTER CHANGE?

By the end of the film, look at how the main character developed and changed from the beginning of the film. Did the character develop or learn? Did they stay the same throughout the film? Include small elements that add up to shape the character.

HOW LONG WILL THE FILM BE?

A good way to judge how long a film will be is by counting the pages in the script. Usually, one page of a script is one minute of a film. This method usually works although it depends on how large the words are. While I am writing my script, I keep the number of pages in mind, which helps keep the script from getting too long or even too short.

SHOW, DON'T TELL

A really great tip I have learned when it comes to making a film or writing a script is "show, don't tell", meaning exactly what it sounds like. Instead of orally saying or narrating lots of details in the film, I try to *show* it being done. For example, if a character is scared of a monster chasing him, he would not say, "I am scared of the monster chasing me!", or a narrator would not say, "Billy was scared of the monster". Instead, it would be shown by his running and panicking. Of course, Billy might also scream, which although is telling he is afraid, it is not directly saying, "He is afraid of the monster." This is a basic example, but it also applies to little details you may not notice when writing a script, especially one with a narrator. I have thought about this tip, and many times it has helped me make my script stronger. Actions and images can replace dialogue.

You may have noticed, many animated short (and some full length) films do not have any characters talking in them. Instead, everything is shown. This is a great example of showing rather than telling while still having a story.

WILL MY CHARACTERS TALK?

Since a short film does not really require dialogue, I always decide beforehand if I want my characters to talk or just act out parts. I usually will include some sort of dialogue in my films as I like giving the characters a unique voice. However, when making a stop motion, you want to decide if your characters are going to actually be moving their mouths as they speak or if words are just going to come out of them without movement.

Back when I only made stop motion videos with my toys, they talked and their mouths never moved. That was okay as most stop motion videos with toys are expected to be like this and still are very much enjoyed. However, when I first began creating my own puppets, I had the option of making functional mouths. I decided my first puppets would not have functional or moving mouths, but I still wanted there to be speaking; I just had my puppets act out the scenes while a voice narrated it. It also made sense for my particular story.

When I actually want my characters to speak, it is more difficult. There are a few options that I use for stop motion:

- Create many removable heads or mouths with different mouth positions
- Simply do not have the puppets move their mouths while speaking
- Hide the puppet's mouth while speaking (close up on their eyes or other objects when they talk, turn their back, and show more than tell)
- Create a functional mouth on the puppet

I will talk about puppet making later, but it is important to know while writing the script if the puppets are going to talk or move their mouths. It is fine if they do not, but you can take the extra steps to make your puppet's mouth move if you want.

WRITE THE SCRIPT REALISTICALLY

Sometimes the story can get out of hand when writing the script. I try to make sure I am willing to animate and create everything I write in the script. For example, I will not write that a character does a backflip unless I am willing to practice and figure out how to make the puppet do that, or I will not make a giant volcano erupt unless I actually want to build a giant volcano. That means I should be willing to take the time and patience to do everything in the script. If I want something to be done, I will work on it until I have achieved it, but I try not to get carried away with special effects, action, or even the amount of dialogue. Try to challenge yourself, but be realistic. Challenging yourself can make your film appear much more exciting and helps improve animating skills.

SPECIAL EFFECTS

I hardly ever will add in computer generated effects. Instead, I physically create the effect in the film using real things. The reason is mainly because I do not use software that allows me to do this. I also think seeing something being made that is real is even more appreciative to myself and my audience. If you want to include special effects in your script, just make sure you have editing software for that. However, do not get carried away adding things to your script that you will not be able to add in later, especially when it comes to special effects.

REVISING THE SCRIPT

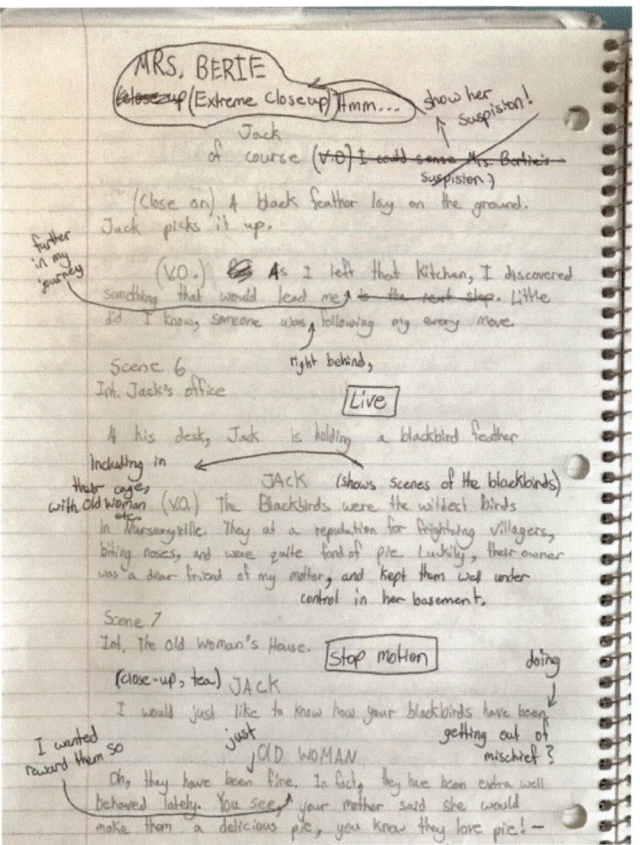

It can take a while to get a good script. In fact, until the end of the entire film process, the script is never really finished. Things will probably change along the way, but it is important to know when the script is good enough to start working with. One way to do this is allowing someone to read your script. Sometimes, I ask people for their opinions on certain scenes in my film. I will not change something just because someone else says I should, only if I think it will make the film better.

I usually will write the first draft of my film, work on sets or props for a while, and then go back to the script to edit it. Taking a break from my script makes me see it in a fresh way, and it helps decide on what I want to change when rewriting. Sometimes if

I am making sets or props and realize I do not have the right materials, or it is not working out, I will change little parts in the script to fit what I have.

When I do come back to revise the script, it is basically deciding what I want to keep or put in the film, and adding words or actions to fill gaps. I also decide if the film has enough elements that help out with the story and give it a bit of variety. I try to make the challenges faced by the characters more difficult. One main thing I think about is if the characters are relatable to real life, but something happens to them that is more exciting than average. I want the script to show this.

Make sure you see your story and film as one, and make all the little pieces come together to bring out your message and idea.

STORYBOARDS

A storyboard is a drawn version of the film with each shot drawn and labeled. The storyboard does not have to be extremely realistic; it can just be drawn using stick figures or simple images, which is less time consuming. Another option is taking pictures of toys or even the actual puppets (if they are complete) acting out each part.
Especially for bigger projects,

storyboards are very useful to keep track of the film, shot by shot, and display your vision of the film. They are also used for deciding and seeing the camera angles of the film, and they are an important step and tool for animating. If you do not have time to experiment too much on set, storyboards are very helpful. They also are great when working in a group so everyone can see how the film will look. Below are some different shots, which you can incorporate in your storyboard and refer to while animating.

CAMERA SHOT SIZES, ANGLES AND MOVEMENT

Here are some basic shot sizes (how much of the scene is in the picture), angles (how the camera is positioned), and camera movements (how the camera moves):

Close-up shot: The subject's face is taking up most of the picture.

Extreme close-up shot: this goes even closer than a close-up, usually showing the subject's eyes.

Wide shot: this is good for setting the scene.

Medium shot: the camera goes closer than a wide shot.

Making Stop Motion Films

POV: a point of view shot is when the camera shows the shot through the eyes of the character. Here, I was moving the camera across the ground as if it were the character's eyes.

Over the shoulder angle: this is good for conversations.

Eye level angle: the camera faces straight ahead at eye level.

High & low angles: a high angle makes the subject look small and helpless. A low angle is the opposite, where the camera points from the ground, and up, making the subject look big.

Zoom movement: take pictures as you slowly zoom the camera in or out.

Pan & tilt movement: a pan is when the camera slowly moves to the side, taking pictures for each movement. A tilt is when the camera moves up or down.

BUDGETING A SHORT FILM

DETERMINING WHAT I NEED AND HOW MUCH IT WILL COST

While budgeting my film, I think about what I will need to make and do everything. Since I work with miniature items, my budget is usually very low for all my films. Most of my supplies and equipment come from what I already own or items that I recycle and create into something new. Unless something is very important, I try to use the leftover supplies from previous projects or items I find at home for my next films. My budgets are usually around $0-20. It is important to think about what I really need to buy and what I could just make myself. Making something that usually would be bought can become a very creative process, and it may even look better than the store bought version. I do not count items that I already own as part of my budget, only ones that I need to buy. However, if I happen to buy something new (like a camera), I would need to add it to the project's budget, even if I will be using it more in the future.

To budget a short film, I usually will make a chart of the things I *need* and the things I already *have* for supplies and equipment. I try to narrow this down until I only have listed exactly what I need. I also set an amount of money for my budget, and I find out how much money everything will cost before shopping. On the following page is an example of what my chart may look like.

After making my chart and including everything, I will add up the costs and see if it either follows with my budget or is reasonable.

Materials	
Need	Have
Yarn: for hair	Hot glue and glue gun
Wire: for puppet armatures	Some cardboard
Fabric: for puppet's skin.	Some fabric
Clear drying glue	Stuffing
Cardboard	Felt
Red, white, light blue, dark blue, and orange paint	Paperboard
Wooden beads	Some paint
Glue stick	Craft sticks
	iPad
	Stop motion app

Even if I am under my budget or above my budget, I always see if I can make do with what I have, without buying something. For example, let's say my need list says *scrapbook paper*. I could possibly make this myself using either the computer or drawing or painting plain paper.

Sometimes not everything can be supplied using what you already own. A few things may be required to purchase at the store. Also, I may decide that buying something will work better than making it, depending on the project or thing I am making. It is important to not get discouraged because of your lack of materials. I used to (and sometimes still do) get very frustrated when something does not work out just because of my materials and equipment. Work with what you have and your final result will be extra special because of this. That does not mean I don't buy things like glue or paint; it means I look at what I have and see what I could make.

SETS, PUPPETS, AND PROPS INTRODUCTION

Still in the preproduction stage, after writing the script (or even before the script is finished), I will begin my favourite part, which is making sets, puppets, and props. I usually make all these things using recycled items or common items from the craft store. I like to keep things cheap, but still take things to the maximum level, depending on the time and supplies I have. I learned a lot about crafting from watching videos and by trying things out with different materials.

PUPPETS

I have experimented with several different styles of stop motion puppets, each made of different materials, and each having a different look. The type of puppet depends on what goes best with the story. For example, if I were trying to make my puppets look fun, colourful, or cartoonish, I would choose the right materials to achieve this look.

I first look at the sketches of my characters and label each part, saying what everything will be made of. I also try to draw the characters as if they are already made of the materials I am going to use.

I often work with fabric, felt, and paper, and I am beginning to work more with clay. Here are some puppet methods I have created using various materials:

Fabric Puppets

This method involves forming a wire armature (skeleton/frame), wrapping it with yarn for extra support, and then covering it with sewn fabric pieces to form the body and head. The facial features may be painted or embroidered on, and the hair is usually yarn that is glued on the head.

Felt Puppets

This method is best suited for puppets with a more fun and colourful look, but it also depends on how the materials are used. The puppets are made with a wire armature, yarn hair, and felt or embroidered facial features. Clothing can be fabric or felt, but the material must be flexible and thin enough to be moved. Usually, from my experience, felt puppets do not take as much time to create, and are great for films with several puppets. Felt animals are also great, since the material is a bit fuzzy. No hemming or turning the felt over is required as this material does not fray and is usually too thick to hem anyway. Although, raw edges may stretch.

Paper Puppets

This method involves creating characters out of pieces of paper, card stock, or poster board. Separate pieces are cut out for different facial expressions and joints such as arms and legs. This method is best for making a stop motion when working with a flat surface, or the puppets can be used upright with a paper stand.

Origami

I also sometimes create things such as animals using origami techniques. These are usually characters that I need a lot of, like butterflies or birds, for example. However, origami techniques may be used for an entire film, if desired.

Claymation

Claymation puppets are made using non-hardening modelling clay over an armature. Very simple puppets with limited movement do not need an armature as the clay is flexible.

Using Toys

When I first started making stop motions, I only used my toys as characters. Using toys is a great way to start out since the characters are already built and ready for the stop motion video. I still built many props and sets for my dolls, and I even made costumes for different stories. When working with toys, it is important to make sure they can move properly. When deciding if a certain toy is right for a stop motion video, you may consider:

- Does the toy have joints?
- Are the toy's joints loose? (Do they stay where they are placed?)
- Is it important for the toy to have many or any joints?
- Can the toy stand on its own, or will a stand or extra support be needed?
- Is the toy large enough to work with, but also small enough to store its sets and props?

When I have decided on the toys (dolls, action figures, etc.) I will be using, I may do some customizing to create the character I want. I sometimes reuse the same dolls for different characters (if I have limited dolls), but I make sure I do some temporary customizing first. I mostly have made my stop motion videos using the same developed characters for different videos, so the stories are more interesting. I usually would not reuse the same dolls in the same series or episodes of my videos.

There are several other methods and materials that can be used to create puppets and characters for stop motion. Pretty much anything can be animated, so use whatever you have. Materials found around the house can be used to make puppets, like toilet paper rolls, recycled paper, cardboard, clay, etc.

PERMANENT TOY CUSTOMIZING

I have done some permanent toy customizing for dolls that I want to have a different look. Customizing may include eye and face repaints, haircuts, and hair recolouring or re-roots. If any toy customizing is attempted, it is important to be very careful as there are a few risks of ruining your toy.

TEMPORARY TOY CUSTOMIZING

I have done a lot of temporary doll customizing, just for fun or for different videos. Some of this includes hair extensions, removable face paint, different clothes, and more. I make all of these things at home from scratch or by using materials that I have carefully tested and ensured were removable. I do a lot of experimenting when it comes to temporary customizing.

After I have decided on how I want to create my puppets, I begin making them. I usually have everything I need right at home. The materials are fairly simple, mostly recycled or easy to find at most craft stores. Before I begin the steps, there are a few things I would like to explain about this puppet making process.

WHAT IS A PUPPET ARMATURE?

An armature for a puppet is everything inside the puppet that makes it function and able to move. This is the skeleton or frame of the puppet. Material (clay, fabric, etc.) covers the puppet's armature to create a moving puppet, ready to animate. The complexity of the puppet's movement is all because of the puppet's armature. As I explain the process of creating a stop motion puppet, I will show how I create my simple yet effective armatures using wire (I have used pipe cleaners in the past, and although it can be a little flimsy, it also works).

HOW LARGE SHOULD MY PUPPETS BE?

Before I make the puppet, I decide how large I want it to be. That includes height and width. If my puppets are too small, it can be very difficult to create and animate. If my puppets are too large, the sets and props will have to be larger, which can take up too much time and storage space. My handmade puppets usually stand anywhere from around 12 ½ cm to 29 cm. Animals/pets can be smaller or larger than the puppets, of course, and paper puppets can be a bit larger as paper is not as difficult to store. Decide on an appropriate height that will be big enough to work with, but small enough to be stored and created. I like to have all my puppets around the same size (some shorter or taller) so that when creating sets and props, they work for most of the characters.

WHERE TO GET CRAFT SUPPLIES

I have mentioned at the beginning of this book that I use a lot of recycled items as my craft supplies. However, I do buy many supplies from the store when needed. I mainly buy my supplies from the dollar store, specialty craft store, and occasionally the grocery store.

I also decide whether it is important for my supplies to be higher quality or to be cheaper quality. Usually, I want my glue to be very high quality as I am using it a lot for important projects and it is what I rely on to hold things together.

I mostly get things from the dollar store. There are many supplies there for cheap that work well. All your materials do not have to be the highest quality to work, so decide what is really important.

MAKING A PAINTING PALETTE

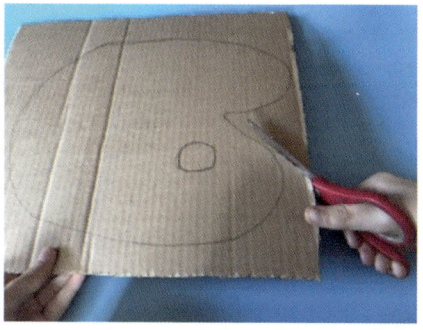  

Although you can buy palettes for painting from craft stores, I have been using a homemade one, which was free. Simply, take a large piece of cardboard, draw a palette shape with a hole large enough for your thumb, and cut it out. Then, you can put paint on your palette. I have been using the same cardboard palette for over a year, and now that it is thickly covered in dry paint, I quickly made a new one.

MAKING THE PUPPET

There are many different materials that can be used to make puppets for stop motion. I usually use fabric or felt, but sometimes I use paper or poster board. Many other materials can be used, such as clay or anything else you have at hand.

On the next page I will be showing the basic steps for making a puppet with a wire armature. Any other material can cover the wire armature, but this is an example using felt.

MATERIALS

- Felt (or other material) for the puppet's skin
- Fabric for the puppet's clothing (something that is thin and flexible)
- Needle, thread, and sewing scissors
- Acrylic or fabric paint
- Small buttons or beads (optional)
- Ribbon, lace, or trim (optional)
- Yarn
- Craft glue
- Wire (sturdy and flexible)
- Pillow stuffing
- End of a paintbrush (for turning the fabric right side out)
- Wire bending and cutting tool(s)

SKILLS USED

- Sewing (if you are using fabric)
- Sculpting (if you are using clay)
- Painting (optional for faces)

Feel free to use the steps on the next page as a guide, and modify any steps to fit the needs of your puppet. For example, if you are creating a claymation figure, the yarn, stuffing, and sewing steps are not necessary.

Making Stop Motion Films

Step 1
Make a pattern for each piece of the puppet's body. Include a border around each piece for seam allowance.

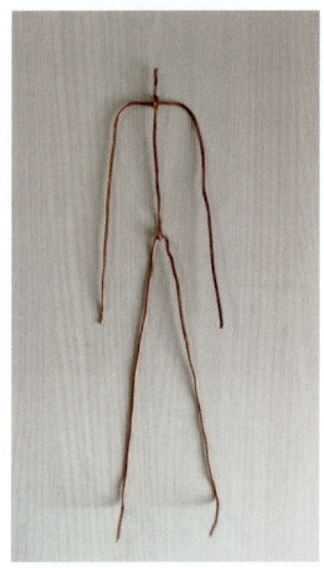

Step 2
Cut three pieces of wire (in total) for the torso, both the arms, and both the legs. Bend the wire and attach it to shape the body. It's okay if the wire is loosely attached.

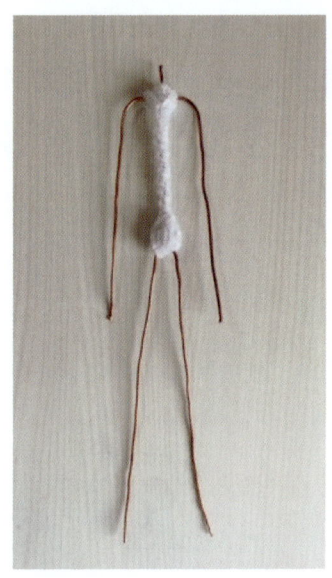

Step 3
Wrap layers of pipe cleaners or yarn around the connected areas of wire to strengthen and tighten it.

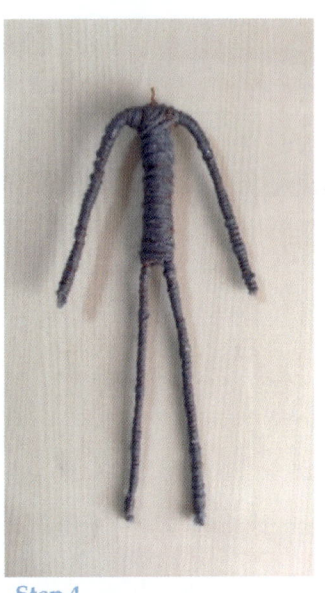

Step 4
Wrap layers of yarn around the wire, adding glue along the way. Add as many layers as needed.

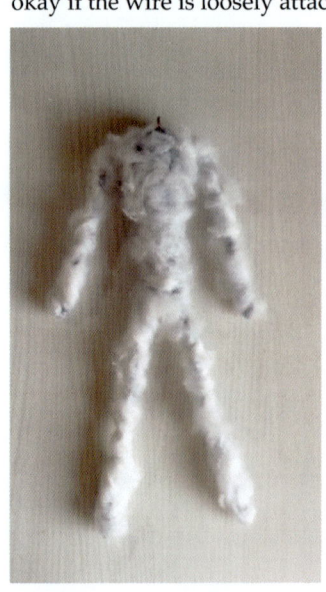

Step 5
Wrap and glue fluff around the body. This step can be skipped by adding extra layers of yarn instead.

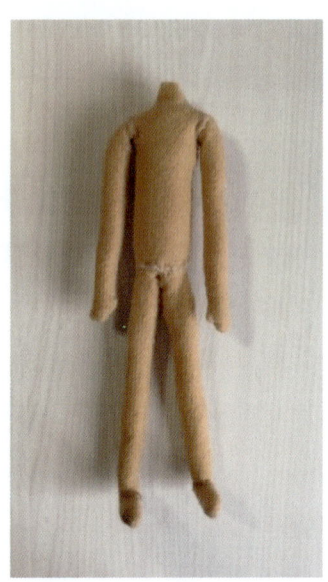

Step 6
After sewing the pieces of fabric for each piece of the body, slide the fabric pieces on the wire body and sew them together to attach.

Making Stop Motion Films

After the body is finished, The head and face are created. The head is usually just two round pieces of fabric that are sewn together and stuffed (middle image). For different puppets, like the Dish (left image) the head may be simply two pieces of poster board. To the right, I made this little mime puppet out of paper rolls and paperboard. The head is just two, rounded pieces of paperboard that I glued together and painted.

TIPS FOR MAKING FACES

When I am making a puppet's face, I try to keep things simple and clear. I do not usually strive for being realistic, but being unique in the faces. I draw out how I want my puppet's face to look beforehand, and then I paint or add details exactly how I have drawn it. It is easy to paint puppets that are made of paper, since if a mistake is made, it can be painted over. However, when painting on the fabric puppets for example, I have to make sure I get it right the first time, so practicing on a scrap piece of fabric is helpful.

There are a few things I do:

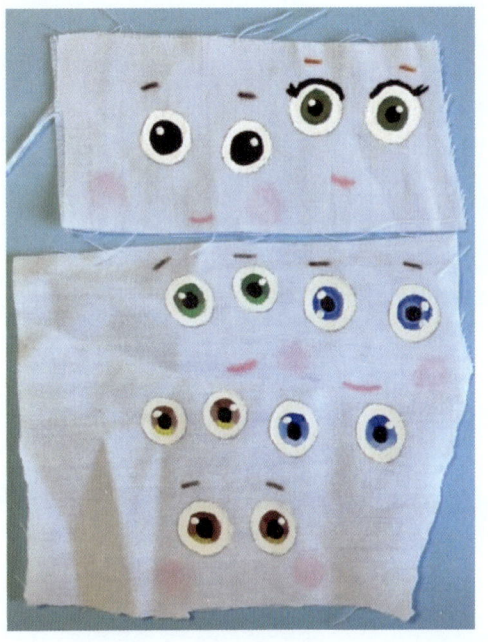

1. Decide on a simple, yet unique face for the puppet. For the eyes, I may choose to use small black buttons, make eyeballs out of beads, or paint simple eyes. You also could use "googly eyes." I will lightly draw the eyebrows using a pencil crayon (coloured pencil), or I will sew or lightly paint them onto the puppet. The mouth can be simply painted, stitched, or drawn with a marker (test it out on a scrap to make sure it does not bleed), and the cheeks can be done using chalk pastels or pencil crayons.

2. When working with felt puppets, it is much more difficult to paint the face as the fuzzy material mixes with the paint. For this reason, I choose a very simple style of face. I may cut out pieces of felt and glue them on, and paint the iris and pupil, or I may cut out pieces of paperboard, paint them, and glue them to the head. I also create a nose out of felt, and I paint the lips, cut out pieces for them, or sew a mouth. When working with felt, embroidering the face with thread can keep things neat and clean.

3. Of course, painting on paper puppets is probably the easiest way to make their faces. Although I still like to keep things simple with paper puppets, it is much easier to create detailed faces. Using pencil crayons or especially paint works great.

THE PUPPET'S HAIR

I mostly use yarn for my puppets' hair. Several strands can be cut, brushed thoroughly with a brush (I use a doll brush), and then glued to the puppet's head with craft glue. When choosing yarn, I find that loose, chunkier yarn works best. You can find this at your local craft store or the dollar store.

To apply the brushed out yarn to the puppet's head, first brush some clear-drying glue onto the head with a paintbrush, add a few strands of yarn to the head, and continue until the head is full. When the head is full, take another strand of hair, fold it in half, and add glue in between the fold. Once it is dry, open it up, and glue it over the top of the puppet's head for the part. Some tighter yarns do not brush out completely, which leaves the hair a bit more curly. Cut and style the hair as desired. For puppets made of clay, the puppet's hair may also be made of clay.

THE PUPPET'S CLOTHES

I always design a puppet's clothes to fit the character's personality. I will sometimes do research on certain clothing from different times, or I will design something unique.

When making my puppets' clothing patterns, I do something simple that can look much more intricate by adding little details such as ribbon, buttons, or patches of fabric.

I have a large fabric box full of all sorts of fabric that I like to use for my puppets. Most of it was given by my grandma, but other pieces are from my local fabric store, or it came from old clothing and other items. When deciding what to use, I make sure the fabric is lightweight and flexible, so the puppet can still move around in it. I also use a lot of recycled fabric from ripped t-shirts, socks, or old jeans.

For fastening the clothing item when the fabric is not stretchy enough to be pulled over the puppet, I will use Velcro, elastic, or buttons.

CREATING ANIMALS

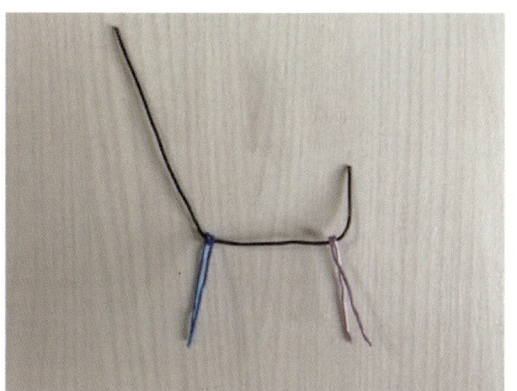

Similar to making a human puppet, animals are made by creating a pattern for each piece of the body. Then, a wire armature is created, like shown earlier. After the pieces of fabric are sewn together, they are placed over the wire.

Making Stop Motion Films

HOW DO MY PUPPETS STAND UP?

It sometimes can be very challenging to try and make your puppets stand on their own. Some objects are already hard enough to be balanced without support, let alone be moved and animated while still standing. Fortunately, I have a few techniques for doing this. The way the puppet is made can have a lot to do with how it will stand while being animated.

USING A STAND

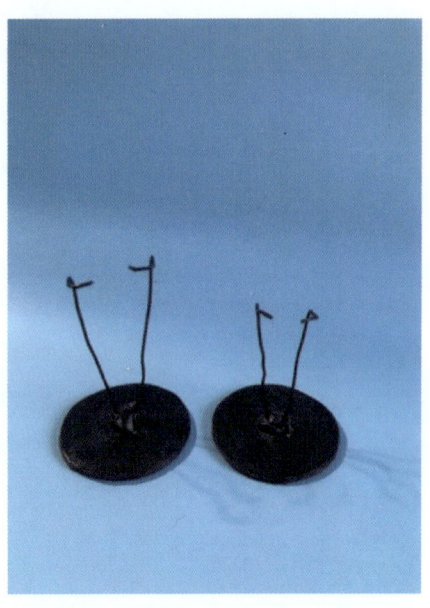

Creating a stand and using it for your puppet works very well, as the puppet can easily be balanced without much struggle. The downside of using a stand is that the puppet's legs must be out of the picture while animating. Another issue is that the puppets sometimes look as if they are "sliding" instead of walking from leg to leg. However, if this is an issue (which it is not always) there are some alternative methods.

To create a custom stand for almost any puppet:

Step 1. Cut several round shaped pieces of recycled paper board (material from cereal or pasta boxes) and layer and glue the pieces together with a glue stick. This is the base of the stand.

Step 2. Take a long piece of thick, sturdy wire and bend it in half, reaching the height of the puppet's waist. Bend the top of the wire to create a round shape that the puppet's waist can be placed and fit into. Heavily and carefully glue the wire to the base using hot glue. You can paint the stand if you want.

STICKY SHOES

This method allows the puppet to stand on its own, but requires a puppet with sturdy legs, and flat, smooth feet. I have used the "sticky shoes" method on my felt puppets as their feet are larger and flatter than fabric puppets. My felt puppets are also shorter and usually wider, allowing better balance.

To animate a puppet using the "sticky shoes" method, follow these steps:

Step 1. Ensure the puppet has sturdy legs and flat, smooth feet.

Step 2. Hot glue a piece of paperboard on the bottom of the shoe, and paint to match the shoe colour.

Step 3. Place a smooth piece of sticky tack or removable tape onto each foot.

Step 4. Test it out by having the puppet stand on the ground, and move its feet around.

This method works best if the puppet is walking on a smooth, flat surface, however, you may try using Velcro on the puppet's feet if it is walking on a fuzzier ground. Adding something sticky to the puppet does not only work well for walking, but also for when the puppet is holding an object or climbing up something.

PAPER STAND

This method of allowing the puppet to stand works well with the paper puppets, like

this flamingo. It is standing up because of a folded piece of poster board that is attached to it. The puppet should be lightweight but not flimsy, too narrow, or tall. Creating this stand is simple:

Glue together a few layers of poster board or card stock, fold it, and glue that to the bottom back of the paper puppet. Paint it to blend in with the scene, like how this flamingo's stand is painted and trimmed to look like grass.

Making Stop Motion Films

OTHER WAYS OF SUPPORT

Besides stands, there are other methods for supporting a puppet or object as it moves. For one of my short films, I wanted a string of origami birds to fly across the sky. Since these birds were going to be in the same scene as puppets that would walk on the ground, I could not simply lie them flat on a table as I moved them around. Instead, I sewed each origami bird to an individual piece of thread and then attached each piece to a cut out circle of poster board. Now, each bird had its own string but was attached to one piece.

I then decided to create my own stand for allowing these birds to move as if they were flying. I drew a sketch of a stand with one piece of layered paperboard outstretched

that the birds could be attached to. There was enough room so that when animating, the stand would be out of the picture and the birds would look like they were flying. The only potential issue with this, is that you will be able to see the strings. I, however, did not mind them as it gave it a playful look that I really like.

The stand also could be adjusted so the birds could turn, go up and down, and of course, move forward.

I made the base by using a piece of wood and cardboard (it needed to be heavy enough to stay down). I then glued a wooden skewer to the base and attached pieces of paperboard to go across. I painted it and hung the paper birds on it.

You can create your own variations of stands to support and create the illusion of flight or levitation.

TESTING OUT A PUPPET

After I have created a puppet, I like to test out its movement and see if I need to change anything, or even replace parts. Once, I made a felt puppet with wire inserted into the arms for articulation, but the wire quickly became lost and unformed inside the arms. I had to replace the arms, ensuring that the wire was thick and secure enough, with stuffing in the space between the fabric and the wire. After this mistake, I now create my puppets with a tight, fully connected wire armature.

To test the puppet, I usually move it around, act out some scenes with it, and see how well it can stand and walk. I also may animate a stop motion clip of the puppet moving.

I also want to make sure the puppet can do everything I want it to do in the script. Sometimes, a puppet may have many limitations, however, I do not want to create an entirely new puppet, so I have to change little things in the script just because of the puppet. Of course, if this puppet is a main or important character, I would definitely replace parts or even create a new puppet rather than change the script. Many professional stop motion movies use many puppets for the same character, but I keep it at one puppet and just replace parts if needed. It all is a learning experience, so keep testing out new ways of puppet making.

Above are some felt puppets, which my brothers made.

SET BUILDING

After puppet making, I move on to set building. Sets can be anything from a bedroom to an enchanted forest. Whatever is in the script usually has to be built. Although I sometimes reuse the same set from a different project, I usually create new sets for all my short films. The reason is because most of my projects are very different from one another. However, I will sometimes create a very simple set that can be changed by using several different props and furniture.

Creating the set itself is usually simple, but it is the props and extra pieces and features that make it look more detailed.

Here is what I usually will do to create a basic room for my puppets:

CREATING A BASIC PUPPET ROOM

This room can be changed to fit the needs of almost any set, from an office to a grocery store. Windows, doors, shelves, stairs, or any imaginable item can be added to create many different types of buildings. I usually create a corner of a room, which is a room with two walls and a floor, but I also sometimes make full rooms with a back wall, two side walls, and a floor. If a lot of space is needed, I recommend a full room, however, corners take up less storage space, are a little quicker to produce, and work well for many different sets.

I have found that sets take up a lot of space. In order to continue making new sets, I sometimes make foldable sets. These are just like the ones I am going to describe soon, but instead of gluing separate walls together, I score (slightly cut a line down the cardboard without going through it all the way) a piece of cardboard so it can fold to form the walls. Then, I add a piece for the floor.

Here is how to make a basic room:

MATERIALS

- Recycled cardboard
- A glue stick
- Paper (plain paper and/or scrapbook paper)
- Paint (optional)
- Hot glue or strong craft glue
- Scissors
- Ruler
- Pencil

Step 1. Measure, draw, and cut out two equal sized pieces of cardboard, a bit taller than the puppet or character.

Step 2. Cut out another piece of cardboard for the floor (must be at least the same length as the bottom of the walls).

Step 3. Cover the pieces of cardboard with paper, using a glue stick, smoothly coating the entire surface with glue. It is important that the paper is attached smoothly to the cardboard, without air bubbles. Make sure to also cover the raw edges for a nice finish.

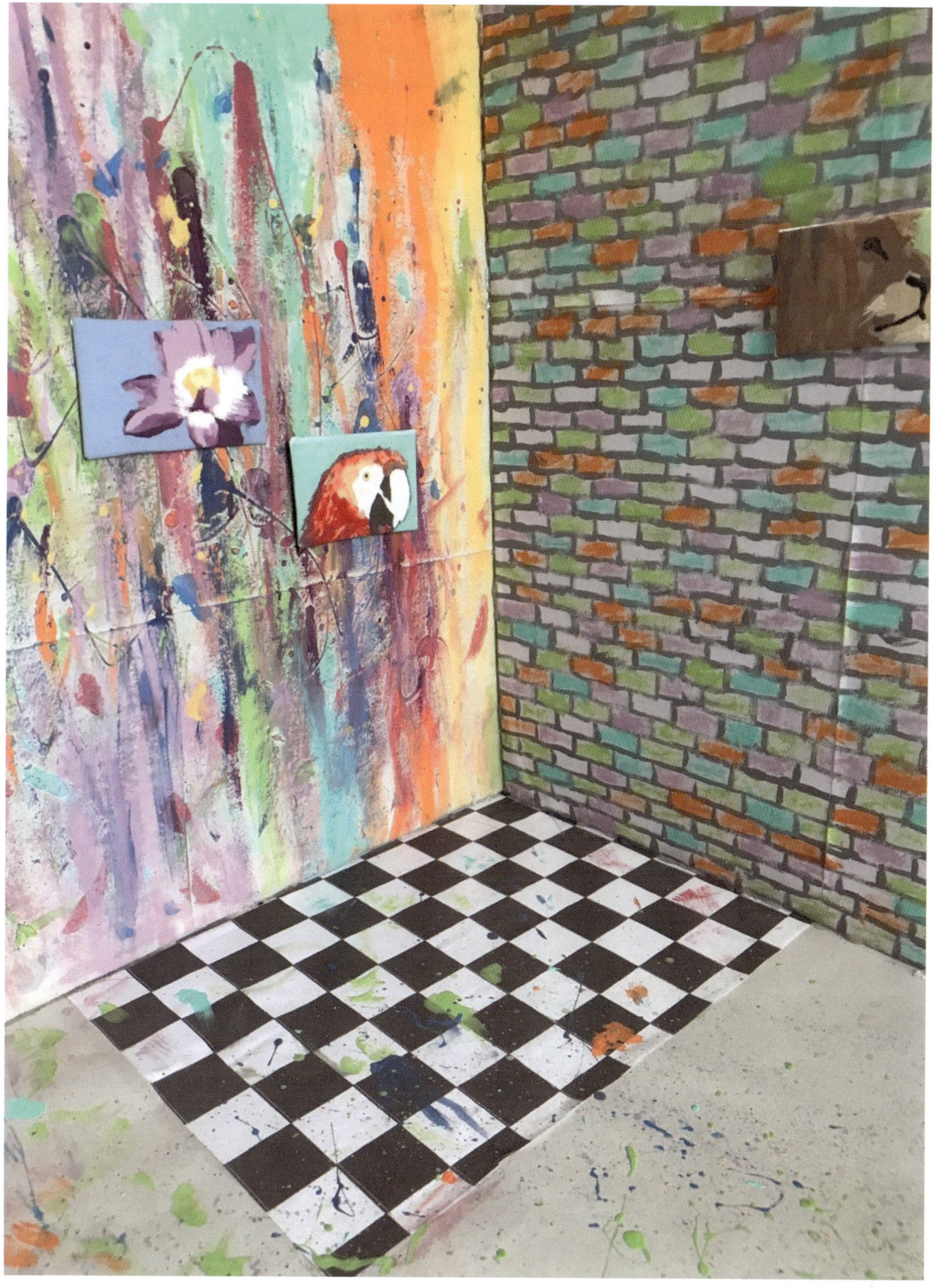

Step 4. Taking the two walls, glue them together at the corners as well as to the floor, using hot glue or another strong craft glue. The room is complete.

If desired, three walls may be included, instead of two, to create a full sized room. To do this, just cut out one large piece of cardboard and two equally sized smaller pieces. Then, cut out a piece large enough for the floor, and continue the rest of the steps.

I like using scrapbook paper in different patterns or textures to look like wallpaper or flooring. If you would like your walls to be white, you may use plain white printer paper. Plain paper can also be painted to create your own designs. Just be sure the paper is thin enough to be bent and glued over the edges of cardboard. You may also glue fabric onto the cardboard for a carpet floor or pieces of cut craft sticks for a wooden floor. I sometimes use floor samples from my local hardware store. The

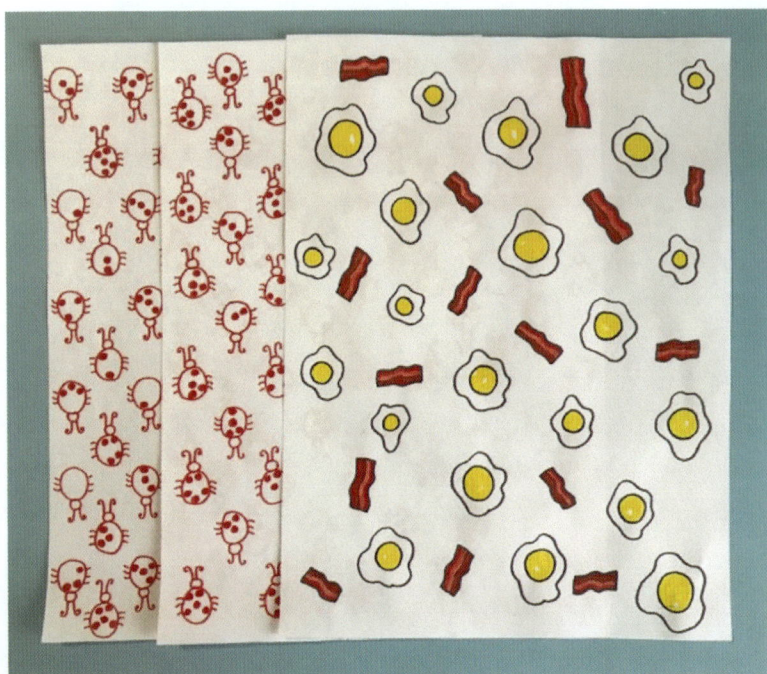

colourful room on the previous page was painted by hand. I started with plain grey paper, added a section of checkerboard floor (which I made on the computer), and then painted the entire room. I even drew out a brick design and filled it in with colourful paint. To the left are some of my fun wallpaper designs. I simply took a plain piece of paper and drew on a design with markers. Then, the wallpaper can be glued onto cardboard for the walls of a room.

EXTRA DETAILS

I like to get creative with my sets by creating slanted ceilings, windows, and doors. A window can be made by cutting a rectangle out of the middle of a wall. I also add in clear pieces of plastic from product or toy packaging for the window, and I add on small strips of white paper. Later, when decorating, I will add on a curtain rod and curtains.

Sometimes, I make one wall shorter than the other, add on a piece of cardboard, and

glue it to both walls, so it is slanted, to create an attic style ceiling.

Shelves can easily be added by cutting rectangular pieces of cardboard, covering them with paper, then gluing them to the walls.

All of these extra features can permanently give the room more detail. Keep experimenting with different methods and techniques.

CREATING A BASIC OUTDOOR SET OR BACKGROUND

Much like the indoor sets, the outdoor sets are a basic and simple concept that really are fully transformed when the props and extra details are added. For my outdoor scenes, I like to use two very large pieces of poster board or cardboard, paint them, and then set them against a wall on a table. It makes it much easier to store as the two pieces are not connected to each other. The main thing about an outdoor scene is that it is very open and large. This method also works well for when you just want to have a background without creating an actual set. You can paint or draw backgrounds to achieve the setting you are going for.

Here is how to make a basic background:

MATERIALS

- Large piece of poster board (in the colour of your choice)
- Large piece of cardboard
- Acrylic paint

Step 1. Choose a poster board for the background of the outdoor scene. For example, if you are creating a sky, choose blue, or you can use white and paint everything over it.

Step 2. Using acrylic paint, paint over the poster board to create your background. It could be anything from an ocean to a night sky. I like to let one coat dry before starting another to prevent the paper from getting soggy. I also like blending the colours as I paint, giving it a natural fading effect.

Step 3. Take a large piece of cardboard and paint it

for the ground of the scene. The ground could be grass, soil, sand, etc. Painting on cardboard can cause the cardboard to curve, so be sure to wait for each coat to fully dry before starting the next. You may also have to put weight on the cardboard to keep it flat while drying.

The poster board can later be taped (using a kind of tape that does not remove paint) or sticky tacked to the wall for the background. The piece of cardboard is placed on a table in front of the background for the ground. You can also use scrapbook paper with photographed outdoor images such as grass, clouds, or water for outdoor backgrounds. I sometimes will take photographs of real outdoor things and print them out for a realistic background. Other times, I prefer the hand painted artistic look over the realistic look.

In the winter scene, I painted the background and ground. Then, I added a piece of clear plastic for ice and white glitter for snow.

Make sure you fill your outdoor set with a lot of items that go with the setting. Here, I created several trees for the enchanted forest by painting twigs and making yarn pom-poms. I also made felt mushrooms and paper bird nests with clay eggs.

Also, if you plan on using a green screen for your backgrounds, you can take photos for this; make sure there is enough space in the background for the characters to walk and move around, without them walking on the sky or something.

CREATING OTHER SETS

Although I have explained the process of creating sets such as simple rooms and outdoor scenes, there are several other types of sets that require different methods. These include things like caves, brick walls, staircases, etc. I will not be explaining the process for each type of set, but I will provide some tips on creating them.

1. **USE CARDBOARD AND PAPERBOARD.** Every set I have made has cardboard as the main material. Pretty much anything can be constructed using cardboard. Pieces can be measured, cut out, and glued together to create several things. Cardboard can be covered with paper and fabric, so you cannot really tell what the item is made of. The best part is that cardboard is a recycled item!

2. **EXPERIMENT WITH TEXTURES.** When creating a set that is part of nature, such as rock, a volcano, or caves, I try to cover the cardboard in some way that gives it a realistic texture. For example, for one of my short films, I cut out hundreds of small rectangles of cardboard; these were layered, painted, and then glued together to form a brick wall. I also used hot glue that I later painted white to look like mortar. Then, I glued moss to the top and bottom of the wall.

When I started crafting miniature sets, after a little practice, I was able to create almost any set I wanted out of cardboard, paper, glue, fabric, and a few other materials. I just need to look at what I have and think of how I could make something. An important thing to take note of is neatness. Being neat, tidy, and taking your time with your work will save you time from going back and fixing or changing things.

LOOK AT REAL PLACES

Looking at real buildings, scenes, or rooms is one of the best ways to create something that looks realistic or just get inspiration. I usually get ideas for my miniature stop motion sets from movies, images, home décor books, or actual places I have seen. I like my sets to look detailed, and seeing the real thing can help you see those details you may not have thought of adding otherwise.

Sometimes I will create something like a prop, clothing item, or set; I later see the real thing, and I will be missing a lot of details I did not think about before. Other times I create something without any guidance, and it turns out unique and creative. I think looking at real things is great for inspiration, but you do not always need to copy exactly as seen. Leave room for creativity when you get the idea.

CREATING FURNITURE

Once a miniature set is complete, I start creating the furniture for the room. These are things like a bed, table, chairs, couch, etc. Again, most of the furniture is made using the basic supplies: cardboard, paperboard, fabric, paint, and wooden craft sticks and dowels. Using these supplies, almost any piece of furniture can be built.

USING CARDBOARD FOR FURNITURE AND APPLIANCES

In most cases, when I am using cardboard for furniture, I cover it with paper or fabric to give it a nice look. While every piece of furniture varies in its process of creation, here is what I almost always do when working with cardboard for furniture:

Step 1. Measure and draw shapes on cardboard that can fit together to form the piece of furniture. For example, if I were creating a kitchen counter, I would cut out 1 long rectangle (tall enough for the puppet) for the front, 2 equally sized rectangles for the sides, and 1 for the top. The bottom and the back of the counter are not necessary to create as they will be touching the wall and floor, and they will not be seen. I also would cut out pieces for faux cupboards and drawers, unless I choose to cut out pieces for a functional counter.

Step 2. After all the pieces are cut out to create the piece of furniture, I individually cover each piece of cardboard with paper or fabric, and I glue these together to finish the piece of furniture.

Step 3. Add any extra details. I sometimes will paint the piece of furniture when it is covered in paper, depending on the look I am going for. Otherwise, I will use textured or patterned scrapbook paper. I also like to add trim or ribbon to some other pieces of furniture for more detail.

I sometimes will take an already built box (such as a pasta or small cereal box), and I cover it with fabric or paper to use as a bed or part of a couch. I then may add on extra details such as a headboard (for a bed), or I add armrests and pillows (for a couch). The couch in the picture was made by covering a pasta box and layers of cardboard with fabric. Then, I sewed pillows for the back.

USING PAPERBOARD

Unlike cardboard, paperboard does not have to be covered with paper or fabric. The reason is because paperboard has smooth edges once it is cut, unlike cardboard, which has noticeable rough edges. When using paperboard, the process for making an item is exactly the same as using cardboard, except I just have to cut out several layers of each piece to make it thick enough. I usually use the paperboard layering method when creating things such as tables, some chairs, and other items that I do not want to cover with paper or fabric, but I still want to have smooth edges.

Below are the basic steps I follow when working with paperboard:

Step 1. Measure and draw shapes on paperboard that can fit together to form the piece of furniture or item you are creating. For this mini dollhouse, I drew and cut out pieces of paperboard for the back, sides, top, and for the walls and floors.

Step 2. For each individual piece of paperboard, trace several more layers. Glue each layer together for added thickness and strength.

Step 3. Glue the pieces of layered paperboard to create the object.

Step 4. Paint the finished piece.

Stacking and gluing layers of paperboard does not only work well with furniture, it also makes great props.

USING WOODEN CRAFT STICKS

Sometimes, when I am making a piece of furniture, and I want it to be wooden, I will use things such as craft sticks, large craft sticks, coffee stir sticks, wooden dowels, toothpicks, or skewers. These items can easily be found at the craft store or even recycled from other things. Cutting wooden sticks can be a little difficult. I usually just use a pair of scissors, or I use some old pruners (handle with extreme caution).

Here is how I make furniture using craft sticks:

Step 1. Cut out several pieces of craft sticks, so that when they are lined up, they form a shape for the piece of furniture. For example, when I was creating this bunkbed, I cut out several pieces for each part of the bunkbed. For extra strength, you may stack and layer the sticks.

Step 2. Using hot glue or another strong craft glue, glue the pieces of wood together. If you have a row of individual craft sticks and want to attach them, you can just glue a few pieces of craft stick across the back, attaching them all.

Craft sticks and other wooden materials are great for several things, from tables and chairs, to bunkbeds.

USING PAPER ROLLS

Paper rolls are simply rolled and glued pieces of paper that form cylinders. They can be used for several things such as legs for tables or parts for a mini camera. The process is simple, but once put together and painted, paper rolls can create or be used as parts for anything cylinder shaped.

Here is how I make paper rolls:

Step 1. Cut out long strips of paper (can be recycled) as wide as desired.

Step 2. Place a toothpick, wooden skewer, or dowel (depending on how large your roll will be) at the end of your paper strip. Roll the paper around the object, applying glue as you go. Remove the object, and continue rolling and gluing the paper, until it is the desired thickness. Different sizes can be made and glued together to create a variety of furniture pieces and props.

Making Stop Motion Films

CREATING PROPS AND DECORATING

When the sets and furniture are complete, I begin the long process of prop making and decorating. My favourite part of preproduction is the crafting part, and out of the crafting part, my favourite is the props. A prop is anything that the puppets could possibly interact with or hold during the film. Props can be made of anything, but I like to use recycled items and common supplies that I already have at home or that can be found at craft or dollar stores.

There are so many things that need to be made for a stop motion film. I like all my sets to look finished and complete with all the props, items, or decorations necessary for the film. For a short film, I will make everything from food, stuffed animals, plates, cups, bird nests, trees, mushrooms, and more to fill up a set. Instead of describing every single prop I have ever made, I will simply share techniques, ideas, and supplies I commonly use.

78

MAKING FOOD

Many foods I make are made using one simple recipe that creates a dough-like clay; this can be formed to make many things. I also make miniature food using paper, another method that can be done in several different ways.

USING 3 INGREDIENT CLAY

In the back of this book (page 170), you will find the 3 Ingredient Clay Recipe, which can be made into several food items. This clay air dries smoothly and hard. It may be used to make other items, but I have found it works best with food items. It also is a bit heavy and may crack, so be careful.

Step 1. After I have made the clay, I will shape it into whatever I want. I do not use many tools; I just use my hands, something to roll it out with, scissors, and sometimes a butter knife.

Step 2. I will let the clay dry and harden overnight, before beginning to paint/add details to it, if needed.

The clay will dry a white dough-like colour that is already perfect for many things, such as eggs. However, I do like to use paint and chalk pastels for colouring. I like using chalk pastels for things like bread, which needs a golden brown colour, with smooth blends, to look as if it has been baked. Depending on the softness of the chalk pastel, I will use a paintbrush to apply and blend the colour.

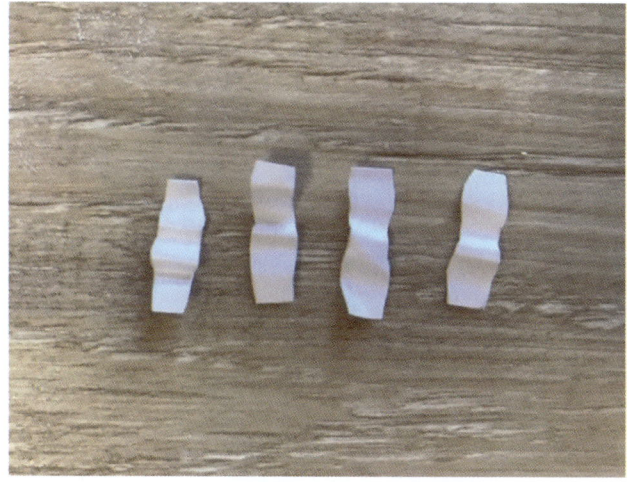

Here is an example of making food using paper. A couple layers of paper were glued together and cut out in shapes of bacon. Then, they were bent to form waves in the paper. Next, the pieces were painted, and several layers of clear drying gloss sealer/glue were added to make the pieces shiny.

SAUCES AND GLAZES

To give food a sauce, glaze, or icing, I like to simply mix school glue with paint; I drizzle or paint this mixture over the food.

MAKING PROPS

Before beginning with making props, I first would like to mention that every prop is different, and every situation is different. I have created many props, and I cannot describe every one of them in this book. Instead, I will be explaining the techniques and methods I use depending on the prop. Most of the time, I will use what I have, or I use recycled items.

DO MY PROPS NEED TO BE FUNCTIONAL?

Like sets and puppets, I always need to decide whether or not something needs to actually work. For example, is it required for a window or a kitchen cupboard to actually be able to open? If the answer is "yes", I will figure out how to do it, and if the answer is "no", I may choose to leave out the extra feature to save time. Even if the prop does not need to be functional, I may add it in just for an extra detail and challenge.

For example, if I made a gum ball machine and was deciding if I needed to make it able to dispense gum balls, I may consider:

- Is the gum ball machine an important part of the film?
- Does the character or anyone use/interact with the gum ball machine anywhere in the script?
- Can I figure out how to make the gum ball machine work?

In many cases, a prop does not actually need to be used. Instead, it is just an extra detail in the background that makes the film more interesting. Other times, it is important for the prop to work or be held/used by the character, even if it is just someone in the background. Here, I made a cuckoo clock, and making the hands able to move was a good detail.

USING RECYCLED ITEMS

I always am on the lookout for interesting pieces in the recycling bin. Besides the usual things I use, such as cardboard, paperboard, and paper, I also try to see garbage in a new way. If something is shaped like a part of something else, I usually will take it and turn it into something new. For example, I found a small glue stick cap, a plastic tube, and a plastic spool; I used those pieces to make a lamp.

Sometimes, little things for creating props are not always found in the recycling bin. Once, when I went to the dentist, and I was allowed to pick some prizes, I carefully looked through the bin for something that could be made into something miniature. I found a little, round, clear container with a red cap. Inside it was a piece of purple fake hair, attached to a clip. I took the container, used it for my gum ball machine, and I used the purple hair for my dolls.

FINDING ITEMS FROM THRIFT STORES

Another place where you can find neat little items for stop motion, whether it is miniature or something that can be made into something new, is at your local thrift store. My sister once found three different miniature tea sets (one is pictured), complete with plates, teacups, a teapot, sugar bowl, and more. I made mini sugar cubes with painted paperboard and white glitter, and I placed a piece of painted paper in the teacup to look like tea. Then, I later featured some of the items from this tea set in a short film.

Sometimes, you just need to see regular things with a different point of view.

PAPERBOARD: FOR ALMOST ANYTHING

I have already talked about using paperboard for making many things, but I wanted to describe how great this recycled item can be. Just by cutting out a shape, tracing several pieces, and stacking and gluing the layers together, I have made so many items, from a cuckoo clock to several cameras. These mini cameras were made by tracing several pieces of paperboard together for the main part of the camera. Then, I rolled small pieces of paper for the lens, and I painted the camera, as well as the details.

Do not get rid of cereal, cracker, pasta, or other product boxes!

WOODEN CRAFT STICKS AND BEADS

I have been collecting and using all sorts of wooden craft sticks and materials for years, which come in several different forms. These are the ones I have used:

- Craft sticks (can be bought at a craft or dollar store, or you can use recycled sticks)
- Jumbo craft sticks (much thicker craft sticks)
- Coffee stir sticks (also known as "skinny sticks", these are thinner and longer craft sticks)
- Wooden dowels, in a variety of sizes
- Wooden skewers and toothpicks
- Wooden beads

I use these items to put together and make several of my furniture items and props, such as a picture frame, crates, clothing rack, curtain rod, tables and chairs, microphone stand, etc.

PAPER PROPS

Several things such as paintings, photographs, newspapers, and paper bags can all be made using paper. For things like books, I will make the hardcover and spine by covering pieces of paperboard with paper, and then I glue in the paper pages. In the image on the next page, I used colourful paper for the covers and glued on cutouts from magazines for the titles of these books. Paper also makes a great material for

things like flowerpots, bird nests, items that use paper rolls, and more.

USING PAPERCLIPS AND PIPE CLEANERS

I often use paperclips, whether they are plain silver, or ones with a colourful plastic coating. I have used paperclips for not only things such as clothing hangers or headbands, but also things like a sink faucet or stove elements. By being bent, cut, and shaped, paperclips are definitely an essential supply, with so much use and potential.

I also use pipe cleaners often, for things like headbands, clothing hangers, and even a pair of glasses, by removing the fuzz. Since paperclips and pipe cleaners are both bendable, they can be made into many of the same things.

For this planet model, I made little planets. Then, after they dried, I painted them, and I used paperclip pieces to attach them. The base is glued together paperboard, which I painted.

Making Stop Motion Films

USING FELT AND YARN

Felt is one of my favourite materials, and I usually use it for many things: clothing items, accessories, animals, mushrooms, boxes, and more.

I also use yarn a lot for a variety of things: scarves, mini knitting kits, puppet hair, and things in nature like trees.

USING CLAY

If I have clay at hand, I like to use it for props that likely could not be made with other materials. Above are some mini rubber duckies I made with natural drying clay that I sculpted and later painted.

Making Stop Motion Films

HOW WILL MY PUPPETS HOLD THE PROPS?

Some props need to be held by the puppets in the film, which can be done a lot more easily with planning and preparation. Some props are easy for the puppet to hold, such as a mug with a handle or a bag. Other things are more difficult, like a spoon or a teapot. I have used a few different methods when it comes to having a puppet hold an item:

- The puppet actually holds the item: This method only works for lightweight items that may have some sort of handle. If my puppet has articulated wrists, it may be able to hold small, lightweight items on its own, without additional support.
- Using sticky tack: I have used sticky tack (and tape) for making my puppets and other characters hold objects, and it has worked incredibly well in many cases. However, it does not work well for felt puppets or some fabric puppets as the tack/tape can tear apart the material.
- Using thread: For my felt puppets, I sometimes will use a piece of thread and a needle to sew an item to the puppets' hands. This method only works with items with a handle or other fabric items that may be too heavy for the puppet to hold on its own. This method can damage props or puppets if used improperly.

This is everything I will be explaining about making sets, props, and puppets. I find this process to be the most time consuming, taking months to create everything for some films.

When I am nearing the end of creating sets, props, and puppets, I usually am near the end of preproduction. For me, the most important thing is that I have made everything in the script as well as all the extra little details, which are not in the script. Before I get into the production stage, I am going to generally explain, on the following page, how I schedule my film.

SCHEDULING THE FILM

Before I schedule or plan certain days to animate a stop motion film, I will take a few things into account, and ask the following questions:

DO I HAVE SCHOOL, ACTIVITIES, OR CHORES ON CERTAIN DAYS?

If the answer is "yes", I will not always animate on these days, especially because I may not have enough time to finish a scene; the same scene done in several different days may look inconsistent.

HOW MUCH TIME PER DAY AM I WILLING TO COMMIT TO ANIMATING?

It all depends if I have something happening on that day, of course. If my day is completely free, I will try to get in as many hours as possible. I sometimes will work on my film for an entire day, although the lighting can change throughout the day, if I am using natural light, which I often do.

HOW LONG DO I THINK MY FILM WILL TAKE TO ANIMATE?

You can predict how long it will take to animate your film based on the length of the script and what is in it. I sometimes will break the script up into pieces, and I decide what I am going to be doing at a certain time. Some shorter scenes are more difficult to animate and take more time than some long scenes. It depends on how much action and dialogue is in a scene.

WHAT IS MY MAIN LIGHT SOURCE?

It is very important to decide where and when I am going to animate my stop motion film; this depends on my light source. I usually film at my desk, beside a window, which produces very well lit scenes at some points of the day. Other times, it is frustrating as the lighting can be very inconsistent, such as if a cloud moves over the sun, and if it is very windy, the clouds are moving a lot. A lot of times, I am animating a scene, and the light in each frame is slightly different. The inconsistent lighting can make an entire scene look like the light is flickering.

Since I am using a window as my light source, I have to schedule my animating to fit the right time of day. I usually cannot take pictures when the sun is setting because the light is very yellow, harsh, and inconsistent. I like to work in the morning after sunrise, and up until the afternoon, as this is when I think the lighting looks best. It is sometimes difficult to do this if I have school during that time. I like to work a little bit after school and as much as I can on the weekend.

Of course, the lighting can be adjusted on the computer during postproduction, but I encourage the lighting to look good right from the beginning.

ANIMATING WITH THE SAME SET ALL AT ONCE

I do not always animate in the order of the script. I usually will set up one set on my desk, do all the scenes with that set, and then move on to the next one. It saves time when moving sets around.

STARTING SMALL

I like to start with scenes that will not be too difficult, and that will help work my way up to the more challenging scenes. This will prevent the film from looking inconsistent in its animation quality as everything will look close to the same level of animation.

An image from a stop motion video by my brother.

PRODUCTION
ANIMATING THE STOP MOTION FILM

At this point, I am finished my script, sets, puppets, and all my props, and I have reached the production step of my film. Production is where I animate all the scenes. (I record the voices in postproduction.)

At the beginning of this book and in preproduction, I explained several important things that would happen in production, such as choosing how many fps to do, how long animating will take, etc. Those were all important things to know before production began. Here, everything should already be planned out, and all I have to do is actually do it. I have the script ready and revised; I have all my props, sets, and puppets ready and working; and, I have a storyboard for my film.

Before I actually start animating and creating my stop motion, I will prepare the equipment I am going to use. In this section, I will be discussing everything I use to create my films, and items I always have handy.

EQUIPMENT AND TOOLS OVERVIEW

I really do not use anything complex or expensive for my stop motion short films. I work with what I have, on a low budget. Here is a list of my usual equipment:

- iPad Mini: I have been using the same iPad Mini for years, and it is still working well. You can also use a camera or a phone. If you are using a camera, you will need a stop motion software on your computer so you can connect the camera to the computer as you animate.

- Tripod: I use a tripod meant for a camera, but I place my iPad on the top, where the camera would usually go (my iPad case has an included foldable stand). Sometimes, I will tape it down for extra support, but it usually balances well on its own. I used to make my own tripod from scratch, which was much less convenient, and sometimes insecure, but helped get the job done for years. You can see how I made my own later in this book.

- Consistent lighting: I make my videos at a desk in my room, beside a window. Although the natural light is definitely inconsistent at times, I plan to do scenes at a certain time of day. I would, however, like to use a lighting set in the future, so I can animate at all times of the day. You can also use the light from a room.

- Desk: It is very important to have a space large enough for sets, scripts, and extra little tools that may be needed. I use a desk in my room that is usually fully dedicated to my film during production.

- Computer: For editing my short films.

- Tape and sticky tack: I always keep a roll of tape and sticky tack (can be found in school supply sections of stores) at my desk for times when I need to attach items, backgrounds, or stabilize something. Note: Make sure to check that the tape does not remove paint or tear apart paper.

Of course, I need my puppets, props, sets, script, storyboard, and other basic items. I also make sure I have any extra devices or stands needed for particular items/scenes.

APPS/SOFTWARES

I have always used free software, either ones that were included with my iPad and computer, or free apps that I download. Here is a list of the apps and software I have been using:

- (Production) Stop Motion Studio app: This app's free version allows you to easily create stop motion videos, edit frame by frame, and export the finished film to your camera roll. No internet connection is required to use this app. There are optional in-app purchases, but I have only used the free features. Things may change in the future, though, (especially with apps and software). I highly recommend this app. Overall, it is easy to use, works great, and everything that I need is free.

- (Production) Stikbot Studio app: I used to use this app all the time as my main stop motion app. Overall, it works well, but I found Stop Motion Studio was smoother. However, this app allows you to use the green/blue screen feature for free, unlike Stop Motion Studio.

- (Postproduction) iPad version of iMovie: My iPad came with a free iMovie editing app that I use to do general editing and recording of my stop motions, before I upload it to the computer. (I will describe more of this process in the postproduction section.) This app works very well for basic editing, just to get everything in order before I fully edit on the computer.

- (Postproduction) Mac version of iMovie: Since my computer already came with iMovie, I have been using it for the final stages of editing. I do not record dialogue for my films on iMovie as I found it to sound sort of echoey and quiet, but I do finish the editing here, by adjusting things like colour, sound, music, etc.

When I first started making stop motions, I did not use an app or software specifically for making stop motions. Instead, I took photographs using a camera or the camera on my iPad, and then I would upload each photo to the computer to edit on iMovie. Next, I would adjust the length of each photo. This way was more difficult to see how much I had moved an object, and how many fps I was doing. Overall, I found using an app worked better, since all the pictures I took went directly into the app as I worked.

Since I currently do not use a camera for creating my stop motions, I do not need to connect anything to the computer while I am animating, or use a stop motion software on the computer. However, depending on what you are using, you may have to connect your camera to a computer as you animate, as I mentioned earlier.

I will be talking more about software and apps when we reach postproduction, however I just wanted to give an overview of everything I use. The only thing I currently use during production is the Stop Motion Studio App.

Keep in mind, things will change over the years. These apps and software I mentioned may not be available in the future, or the costs may change. Find something that works best for you, depending on availability and what devices you are using.

Making Stop Motion Films

SETTING UP AND GETTING STARTED

The first thing I will do is check which scene I will be doing first. It all depends on what I had scheduled, or whatever I think will work best as the first shot. I do not have to animate everything in chronological order as I can later edit it to whatever order I want. I do like to choose a simple shot first, so I can get used to working with my puppets and sets.

THE TABLE

I make sure my table or desk (I mostly use a desk) is cleared and large enough for my sets. I like my surface to be large, smooth, and hard. It is important for the desk to be against a wall, for hanging backgrounds. The area around my desk should be large enough for the tripod or any other equipment. It also is extremely useful for the desk to be near an electrical outlet.

THE TRIPOD

I set up the tripod, which can easily be adjusted for any angle. I place my iPad on the top, using tape to secure it if necessary. I used to make my own tripod, which was less convenient, but it worked for many of my videos and short films. Below I will describe how I did this.

HOW I MADE MY OWN TRIPOD/STAND

Before I used a tripod, I would use several different items each time to build a stand for my iPad; the stand could be put together and taken apart whenever needed. Here is what I usually would do:

Step 1. Find a chair, stool, etc.

Step 2. Place several items on the chair until it is tall enough for the camera to reach the set. I would use many different items for added height, such as books, and boxes.

Step 3. Place the device (iPad) on top of the tripod. You may want to tape your device down.

My iPad case has a foldout stand attached that allows my iPad to stand up. If your device/case does not have this, you can place a heavy object in front of the device for it to lean on (refer to page 111). Just make sure you cannot see the object when the camera is turned on.

Adjusting this homemade stand is more difficult. I sometimes would add or take away books for different heights, zoom in on the screen, or move the tripod back, for different options.

WARNING The homemade tripod/stand method is not always secure, so remember to be gentle when using your device. The tripod may fall over if not stable; therefore, use it at your own risk, and do not leave it unattended.

If you are working with a small set, you can place your camera directly on the table, with a few items to prop it up, instead of using a stand/tripod.

The most important thing about your tripod/stand is that it is stable as you animate!

STARTING TO ANIMATE

After I have set up for my first shot, set up my tripod, and turned on my device, I will open the Stop Motion Studio app, and begin a new project. Then, I go to settings to set the fps (frames per second) to around 15. At the beginning of this book, I explained how to decide what fps you should set your film to.

THE BASICS

Here I am demonstrating how I move this cat puppet. I slowly move it each time, and I curl its tail. Although there is more to learn, and different techniques for more complex movement, these are the general steps:

Step 1. Position the camera to the angle you want. Make sure everything is stable.

Step 2. Take the first picture.

Step 3. Move the puppet very slightly, as if it were one small step to a larger movement, such as walking across the room.

Step 4. Take a picture.

Step 5. Repeat until the puppet has finished its complete move for that shot.
You can practice moving toys or your puppets before starting your stop motion. Try to simply move your puppet across the table before moving on to more difficult things.

Remember to take a lot of pictures, because anything extra can be cut out later!

On the next page are some images from my film where I created a scene of the cow jumping over the moon. The scene was done using flat, 2D characters on a table. The process was similar to the steps above. I moved the paper characters, and I switched out pieces when necessary. You can see the moon has slightly opened its eye, and the cow is mooing. I simply put pieces of paper over the characters for this. It is much easier to balance the characters when they are lying flat. Also, note that the camera needs to be positioned higher up, showing the table directly. It was more of a challenge for me, and it required a very interesting camera setup, using several objects to prop it up in that position. Be extra careful!

Making Stop Motion Films

MOVING THINGS SLOWLY

The less things moved at a time, and the more pictures taken, the smoother and longer the scene will go by. It sometimes is difficult to move the puppet as little as I want to as things lose balance, fall over, or loose joints can drop during a shot. Much of what is done in production is relying on what was done in preproduction, but there also is a lot I deal with during production, too. There are challenges that I may not be prepared for, but I need to solve them. However, in most cases, I try to move my puppets a very small amount at a time. Especially when working with a higher number of fps, things move much faster, requiring more frames to get the same amount of animation as a slower moving animation with less frames. Just remember as you go, things are going to look a lot faster when you watch the scene.

Above are some images from a paper stop motion my younger brother made.

WORKING WITH THE SET FPS

When I was working with a lower number of frames per second, such as 6, I did not have to take as many pictures or move the puppets as slowly. The reason was because the video would play much slower than, let's say 15 fps. Even if more pictures were taken, things would be very slow with a low number of fps. That being said, if I set my fps to a higher number, I have to take more pictures. The reason is because things are moving faster. Especially with a higher number of fps, I try to move things as little as possible each time. When on a lower number of frames per second, less pictures are required to get the length of animation needed. However, if the puppets are being moved too much each time, the video may look choppy or jerky; this creates more of a fun look, but it may not always be what you are going for. To make sure I am on the right track with my puppets' movement and the number of frames per second setting, I will play the video after completing each shot, making adjustments as needed. You will better understand this once you get started.

MAKING SURE THE SHOTS ARE LONG ENOUGH FOR DIALOGUE

Like I said, I always play my finished scenes to make sure they look smooth and are the right length. A very important thing to do is read your script as you go. Sometimes I make things up as I go along, but I usually know what I am going to do before I jump into anything. I will play bits of the videos, making sure they are long enough for voices to be recorded and lined up during that time. Most animated films record the dialogue before animating, but I have found it is easier to match up the recordings to the animation, rather than the animation to the recording. Sometimes, I realize the dialogue is just too long and unnecessary, so I will cut out parts, being sure to write down the changes on the script for later. Other times, I realize there is a gap,

and more dialogue is needed. Even if my puppets do not talk, I still need to make sure things are going at the right speed to tell the story.

ONLY MOVE WHAT IS NECESSARY

A very important thing about stop motion is that only the required and necessary things are moving. That means I am careful to not accidentally bump other items while animating, or move my puppets unnecessarily. For example, if a puppet is stirring a pot of soup, I would try to focus on animating the stirring, and I only have the other parts of its body move naturally. Unless, of course, the puppet is occupied with something else while stirring the soup.

UNNECESSARY PICTURES WITHOUT MOVEMENT

When I first started making stop motions, I knew that more pictures meant the smoother the video would be. That is true, just as long as things are being moved for each frame. I used to sometimes move an object, take a bunch of pictures, and then I would move the object again. I thought this would make it smoother, but really it just made the movement look slower and choppier—as if I had set my fps to something lower than it was. Unless you want something to be a little bit slower or paused, the puppets should be moving a tiny bit each time a picture is taken.

CHANGING THE CAMERA ANGLE

While you are animating each scene, you may want to change the camera angle for a certain amount of time to draw attention to different things you are animating, as illustrated in your storyboard. Make sure you spend enough time for each shot so the audience can focus on what you are trying to show. (Look back at pages 36-37.)

PAUSING/FREEZING A FRAME

Pausing a frame can be done as part of postproduction, but I usually do this as I go, if needed. Pausing a frame for a certain amount of time is good if you want to focus on a character or something, without any movement. Pausing/freezing a single frame is basically the equivalent to taking several photos of the same thing, only it takes less time.

KNOW WHAT YOU ARE GOING TO MOVE BEFORE MOVING IT

To avoid being stuck or unsure where my puppet should go, I always read the script and follow along with the storyboard; then, I know exactly where and what my characters are going to be doing in the scene before I move them. For example, I would first determine that my character is going to "scratch his head" before I begin moving the puppet.

WHAT IF I ACCIDENTALLY MOVE SOMETHING WRONG?

Many times, I have had to fix a mistake, such as bumping an item, or having my puppets fall over during a scene. This can happen often, since everything is very small and sometimes difficult to avoid bumping. There are a few ways to prevent frustrating things like puppets and props falling over or being bumped.

HOW TO PREVENT MISTAKES

- Roll up your sleeves
- Use open, large sets with lots of room to work with
- Ensure everything is in a secure position before starting and that the security will continue throughout movements
- Glue items (that do not need to be moved) down to the set

HOW TO FIX MISTAKES

While it is sometimes difficult to fix certain mistakes, there are a few things that have worked for some situations:

- Re-lineup the puppets or props: Most stop motion apps have a feature that allows you to see where everything was since the last picture was taken. This effect is usually called an "onion skin" effect. I always have this feature enabled, so I can see where things were last placed. Sometimes, I can line up an object perfectly to match the last frame, other times it is nearly impossible. In the picture, you can see a transparent image of where the penguin was before it was moved. The onion skin effect can be useful for when things accidentally fall over.

- Switch to a different shot (angle or shot size): This only works in times when the camera has already shown enough with a certain shot, and something else needs to be brought to attention. I would not do this if the last shot was only briefly shown, or if I still need to show something using that shot.

REDO SCENES WHEN NEEDED

Most stop motion animators do everything in one take. There is not enough time to redo things when it already has taken so long to complete. If you are just making stop motion short films at home, it likely will not take several years to make, so sometimes it is more practical to just redo a couple shots. I sometimes just have to face the fact that I need to redo a shot or scene. It is better to redo something if there were any noticeable mistakes than to keep it. Animating may take longer, but it all is worth it in the end when your film looks the way you want it to.

PRACTICE/TEST SCENES

I always try to be prepared to avoid redoing anything. Stop motion takes time and patience, and a lot of it; however, since I am working on short films, I have a little more time to experiment and redo things, if needed. This is unlike if I were to make a bigger film, where everything must be very precise. I sometimes will practice a shot a couple times before it is good enough, if I am struggling with a particular scene.

Making Stop Motion Films

THE PUPPET'S MOVEMENT AND EFFECTS

In this section, I will be describing how I do certain movements for my puppets, such as running, hair blowing, talking, etc. I also will explain other stop motion effects, lighting, and more.

RUNNING

If my puppet is running or moving quickly, I will first make sure the body is moving naturally. Second, I set the fps to a higher setting to make it go faster, or I take less pictures. Setting the scene to a higher number of fps works well for faster movement, but just make sure you do that scene in a separate project since some stop motion apps will change all of the project's fps, not just one particular shot or scene.

HAIR BLOWING

One of my favourite things to do when moving my puppets is making their hair or clothes blow. For making a puppet's hair look like it is blowing in the wind, I like to

use puppets with yarn or stiffer hair. Yarn is great because it moves easily and stays where it is placed. To make the hair blow, I simply move the hair in the same direction each time I take a picture, as if the wind is blowing it. Blowing on the hair with your mouth can move it more gently. For clothing, do the same thing: move the fabric in a certain direction for each picture to look like it is blowing around.

TALKING

Not all of my puppets move their mouths. In fact, almost all of my puppets do not move their mouths or eyes during the film. I have made puppets with working mouths and paper puppets with swappable facial features, but I am still experimenting with more movable faces. When the puppet is talking, it is important to know how the mouth will move for each word. Saying the word aloud and understanding where the mouth will move each time is important.

Making Stop Motion Films

For paper puppets that have swappable mouths, I will do the following:

- Stabilize the puppet's body.

- Switch the facial pieces every couple frames, using the right pieces for different words and sounds. Make sure to gently press on the pieces and gently remove them, without making the puppet unnecessarily move.

- Next, watch the finished shot and make sure the words fit in with the animation.

For any puppet, the process is similar. Make sure the words can line up with the animation. If your puppet's mouth is only limited to moving up and down, you only need to make sure the mouth is held in each position long enough for each word. Here, I made separate pieces of poster board for the Dish's mouth. As I made the puppet talk, I used a small piece of tape (sticky tack also works) and gently pressed the next mouth position onto the puppet. I held each mouth position for about 2 frames, but do whatever looks best. You can also do this when the puppet is blinking.

MAKING THE PUPPET HOLD AND PICK THINGS UP

When it is time for a puppet to hold or pick up an object, I will usually place a small, flat piece of tape or sticky tack on the puppet's hand. As mentioned earlier, this method does not really work for felt puppets as the material may tear apart. I may place the tape or sticky tack on the puppet's hand before I start the shot, making sure it will not be visible. Then, just like normal, I slowly move the puppet's hand to the object, and gently press the tape or tack onto the object, allowing the puppet to pick something up. I make sure the item is lightweight and sticks well with the tape, without getting damaged.

Sometimes, the puppet can hold an item without any support by bending its wrist and holding the object in its hand.

I also mentioned earlier that I might use a piece of thread sewn into my fabric or felt puppet's hand, wrapping the thread around the object's handle so it can be held. I will always begin a new shot for this as it is very difficult to sew into the puppet's hand while still keeping everything motionless on camera.

OTHER EFFECTS

In this section, I will be describing how I move items and puppets for different effects such as levitation, flight, water pouring, using green screen, etc. I like to try out different things with stop motion, and make my effects in real life. Although it is more difficult for things like rain falling, or water pouring, I do my best to figure out how to physically do the effect.

FLIGHT

There are a few ways I make my characters and objects look like they are flying that does not require the computer.

1. Hand Held Flying: This method involves holding the puppet's legs, outside of the camera image, while the rest of the puppet's body is shown on camera. Since things can get shaky, as it is difficult for your hand to hold still, I sometimes rest my arm on a stack of items while holding the puppet up. Once the puppet is held using one hand, I move slightly, and press the camera button with the other hand. You can also put the camera on a timer to make things a bit easier. When the puppet has moved enough, I will switch from

holding the puppet's legs, to holding its head. The camera should be zoomed in close enough to prevent your hands from being visible.

2. Strings and Stands: I have used strings for lighter objects such as birds, to make them look like they are flying. Instead of attaching long threads to the ceiling, which would get tangled up and are difficult to move, I use a stand that I created specifically for my birds to fly. After the characters are attached to the strings, the stand is simply moved to make the characters look like they are flying. You could also try using a clear plastic stand/stick with the character attached to it to look like they are flying or floating.

3. Lying Objects on the Ground: Objects can appear as if they are flying or floating by lying them on the ground with a flat background. Set the camera directly above the scene and move the characters. Paper stop motions are done like this, but other 3D objects also work.

LIQUID POURING

For some of my videos or films, I want to show something like a pot of tea pouring into a teacup or a tear falling from a character's eye.

Doing this is fairly simple as all I need to do is create pieces of painted paper (or clear plastic) and move them to create the effect desired. For example, if I were to make a pot of tea pour, I may watercolour paint a piece of paper in the shape of pouring liquid; I make several other pieces of paper in the shapes of each stage of the pouring. Then, I would attach the pieces of paper onto the pot, using tape or sticky tack. Next, I would tilt the pot while I switch the pieces of paper for the different stages of pouring.

Here, during an interview, Humpty Dumpty was nervous, so I placed a small piece of watercolour painted paper coming from his forehead to look like he was sweating. Then, I slowly moved the paper down his head as I took the pictures. The paper was light and it stuck to the felt material of the puppet, so it was easy to attach and move.

If you want a lot of water in your film, you could try using plastic wrap, clear plastic from packaging, and water patterned paper.

GIVING YOUR CHARACTERS PERSONALITY THROUGH BODY LANGUAGE

In preproduction, I talked about giving your characters personality while writing the script, and here I will be explaining how to show characters' personality through their body language.

A lot can be said about a person simply through their body language and actions, which is why many short films do not have any dialogue; they rely on just actions, sounds, and music to tell the story. Even for a short film that has a lot of talking, body language is still essential. In fact, it can sometimes be even more important than words. Some words in a script can be replaced with movement instead. Although I do like to include dialogue in my films as I feel it enhances the story and is fun to do, I try to take extra time to work on the body language.

Some examples of body language:

- Scratching your head in thought
- Rubbing the back of your neck when nervous
- Gesturing with hands while talking

USING A GREEN OR BLUE SCREEN

Although I do not use green screens for my backgrounds as much as I used to (I mostly paint my backgrounds now), I will be explaining how I have used the green screen effect in the past.

Since the Stop Motion Studio app does not include a free green/blue screen feature, I have used the Stikbot Studio app for this, and it has worked smoothly for the most part.

A bright green or blue sheet, poster board, or background is required. I used to use a bright green shower curtain from the dollar store, green poster board, green pieces of cardboard, and even sometimes a bright green yoga mat. Occasionally, I would use bright blue backgrounds for a blue screen when something I was using was the same colour as the green screen. I tested out my background by placing it in front of the camera to see how well it changed to a new background. Note: if you are using a blue screen, just make sure the app is set to the blue screen setting. It is important that the scene is well lit, so the colour looks bright green and not too pale or dark, due to different lighting.

The Stikbot Studio app includes several backgrounds to get started with, but you also can take your own photos to use for backgrounds, which I did for backgrounds that the app did not provide. The new image will appear on your screen, so it looks like your characters are in a different place, and you can continue your animating as normal.

Here are my pros and cons of using green/blue screen:

PROS
- You do not have to build as many sets
- You can use any image of your choice to switch the background
- You can create many effects and illusions
- You can simply create any world

CONS
- The lighting needs to be perfect

LIGHTING

It is very important to think about the lighting while making your film. Although the lighting can be fixed and edited later, things should still look good from the beginning, without relying on technology as much. The light from my window produces clear, natural light during the day, and yellowish light in the evening. I like the lighting to look natural and soft, not too harsh, bright, yellowish, or blue. To achieve this, I need to work on my animating at the right time everyday.

FINISH THE ENTIRE SHOT OR SCENE AT A TIME

When using natural light that is uncontrollable and inconsistent, I try to finish an entire shot or even scene all at once, without stopping and coming back the next day. The lighting can look very inconsistent at a different time or even same time of a different day. If I ever have to come back to do the same scene on a different day, I make sure it is the same time, and I compare the lighting to make sure it looks similar. However, it is extremely important to finish the entire shot or scene all in one day, preferably not during sunset or sunrise, when the light will be constantly changing.

If you are using artificial light for your entire film, you will have more freedom and time to finish a shot without the light changing. It is still important, though, to finish a shot in one day as the items, camera, and angles may be slightly moved the next day.

NIGHTTIME SCENES

Even if a scene is supposed to be set during the night, I still animate it during the day with a well lit set. I do this for two reasons:

1. My camera is grainy and less clear when it is dark.
2. The light is only going to get darker, making it more difficult to see what is going on.

After I have animated a scene, I will later edit it in postproduction to look darker and more blue. This way, the images are still clear, and I have more control over the lighting. I also use painted night sky backgrounds for outdoor scenes. In one of my short films, my favourite scene was one I animated during the day, but it was set during the night. The curtains in the room for that scene were glowing as if the moon was shining on them. Really, it was the sun shining on the curtains. I don't think I really had to change the colour very much while editing because it already looked like it was during the night. I also think the dark blue sky background that was seen through the window helped create the illusion of night.

During the night, I try not to animate only using the lighting from my room as the main source. The lighting usually looks sort of dark, grainy, and harsh this way. Unless using professional lighting equipment, I think things look best with natural light during the day.

WHAT TO DO WHEN NATURAL LIGHTING IS INCONSISTENT

Several times, I have been in the middle of animating a stop motion when a cloud goes in front of the sun, a cloud moves away from the sun, or the sun is too close to where I am working. When the light is changing so much, each frame looks slightly different and uneven, which causes the final video to flash. When this occurs, the best thing to do is just stop and wait for the lighting to improve, or I move to a different location. It is nearly impossible to later adjust the lighting to all be exactly the same, especially when the differences are so obvious, due to each frame being played one directly after another. When the lighting is changing so much, it is challenging to quickly take each photo with the same lighting as the last.

To prevent inconsistent natural light, I start to animate when the sun is not directly behind my window, but the room is still well lit. Usually, when the sun is directly behind me, the lighting is a little harsh, too bright, or shadowy and any changes will be much more dramatic on camera. However, the sun should not be directly in front of you either.

MAKING A STOP MOTION FILM OUTSIDE

I used to make almost all my stop motion videos outside, before I decided working inside was more convenient in most cases. I would bring all the toys and props needed, and start my video. I made many videos in the spring, summer, and early fall. It is sometimes difficult, but it also can be a lot of fun.

Here are my pros and cons of making a stop motion outside:

PROS
- Realistic outdoor scenes
- Great lighting
- Lots of space

CONS
- Wind blows over puppets and sets
- Ground is unstable and uneven
- Sun fades items

Usually on a clear, sunny day, my stop motion videos worked smoothly, however, I have experienced several minor issues along the way such as items being unstable and falling over, bugs crawling on my equipment, rain, and the sun fading my stuff. Since my videos were not very long or complex, I usually was only outside for a few hours.

I think making videos outside is a great, fun way to get started into stop motion, without having to build very many sets. Just make sure your stuff is not left in the sun for too long and does not get dirty.

TAKE LOTS OF EXTRA PHOTOS WHILE WORKING

When I am creating a stop motion, I will try to take lots of photographs for movie posters and advertising. These could simply be images from the film, or full images for movie posters. I like to take these pictures during production, just in case something gets worn out or damaged after the film is finished. Plus, it saves time and effort from setting up scenes later.

I also may take a photo of a background that will be used for the title at the beginning of the film, or for credits at the end. For example, I used my painted night sky backdrop for the background of my film's title.

Making Stop Motion Films

BONUS FEATURES

As I am nearing the end of my film, or even during the entire production process, I may decide to create extra little videos or clips that can be included as a special feature or behind the scenes videos. These could be things like interviews with the cast, deleted scenes, or even made-up bloopers. I also may take behind the scenes photos of myself working on set. Since these extra features are not officially part of the film, they don't even have to be stop motion, but live action, if time is limited. These are just extra fun things to do when the work is almost or is done.

WRAPPING THINGS UP

A short film can take anywhere from a few weeks to several months to finish animating. I usually know I am done animating my stop motion when:

- I have finished every required scene
- I have carefully watched each finished scene, making sure it is the right length, and there are not any unfixable mistakes (many mistakes can be fixed in postproduction, but not all)
- I have read the script while watching each scene, making sure dialogue can fit in with the animation, or the new updates of the script are recorded
- I am satisfied with each scene
- I have been working on my film for a long time and I do not see anything else that I can do

PACKING UP AND STORAGE

When I have decided I am finished with the production of my film, I will pack up my sets, props, and puppets into a box, and I carefully store them away, making room for my next project. I make a lot of stuff that takes up a lot of space. Here is how I store my stuff, once I have finished:

- Individual Bags: I like storing small props in plastic zipper bags, (ensuring any fragile pieces are wrapped up). If a prop was made specifically for a

particular film, I will store it with the rest of that film's stuff. Otherwise, I store it with my common props and sets, which do not belong to a specific film and usually I use for many projects. I also make sure to label the bags.
- Boxes: After I have placed everything small into a plastic bag, I carefully put everything into a cardboard or storage box, if I have no room on a shelf.

Then, I will store these boxes in my closet or wherever I can find free space.

These sets, props, and even puppets can be reused or modified for future projects, which helps save time and storage space.

QUICK GENERAL EDIT

After everything is cleared up, I do a quick edit of my short film to get everything organized, before the real editing takes place. Sometimes I do this step as I go along with the animating, which is why I am including this in the production section, and not postproduction.

In a general edit, I will first start by arranging things on the stop motion app I have used. I will usually cut out blurry or extra frames, freeze frames I want to be longer, adjust the fps if needed, and switch the shots around, to get everything in order. This step is very important, whether done as you go along, or after animating everything.

POSTPRODUCTION
EDITING, RECORDING DIALOGUE, SOUNDS, AND MUSIC

Postproduction is the final stage of a film. When all the required scenes are animated, I will begin editing. For me, it is usually the shortest stage of my film. The reason is probably because of the simplicity and limitations of my editing software, the length of my film, and the amount of time I take on animating and making sure there are not any noticeable mistakes. I do not like to rely on editing on the computer to make my film look good; I like to start out by trying to make everything look good before I edit.

Generally, postproduction takes about 1-4 weeks for me, depending on how much I am working, and how short my film is. My stop motion videos with my toys only took a few hours to a weekend to edit. During this stage, I edit my film, adjust the colour, select or record music and sounds, and record the dialogue. My film may go from being very long to being a lot shorter, all because of editing. Many times, the shorter the better, if it means the story is told well, without too much extra and unnecessary filling in or scenes that drag on. Essentially, postproduction is a required and important part of any film. It is a step that helps the film flow. Editing assembles the film and polishes it.

EDITING

WHAT DO I NEED?

I use various items and editing resources during the postproduction stage of my short film. I try to keep everything free of charge during postproduction, using tools I already own at the time of my project. Here is what I use:

- Computer

- Editing Software: I use iMovie. This editing software was included with my computer, and it provides the basic tools necessary to create a short film. I also use the iMovie on my iPad for general edits. Use whatever video editing software you have, or look into downloading one.

- USB Storage Device: I use this for storing videos, images, and fully finished projects. Make sure you have something for storing your projects.

- Music: When editing, music is a very important part. I usually will use copyright free and free of charge music from the internet.

- Sound Effects: Everyday sounds are recorded to be used as sound effects for the film. I create sounds for my videos and short films, and then I record them. I also use some effects from the iMovie sound library, although I like many things to sound original.

These are the basics, but I may also use some other items throughout this process.

GETTING STARTED: EXPORTING TO CAMERA ROLL

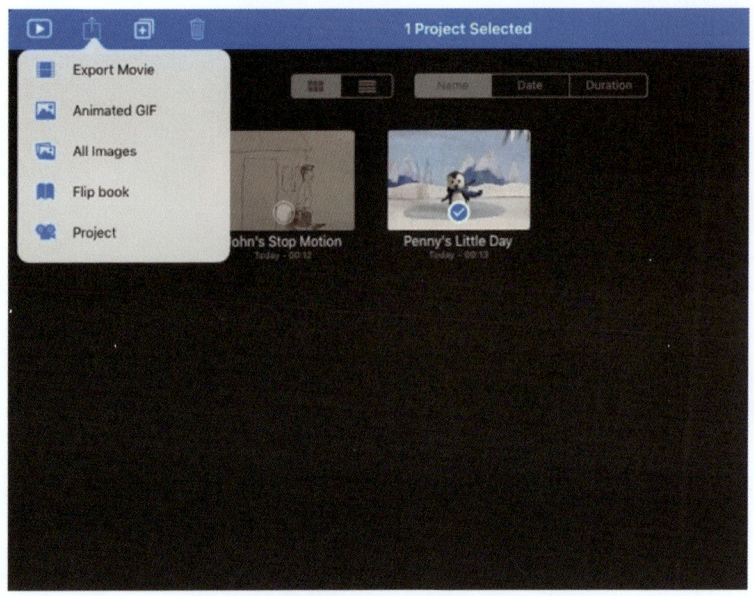

The first thing I do after my quick general edit (on the app) is export everything to my camera roll. Depending on what you are using, this may be found by clicking the "share" arrow icon and then selecting each scene of the project to export to your device's (iPad) camera roll. I try to export to the highest quality, which can take a bit more time, but it is worth the wait. If you have already been animating with your camera connected to the computer, this step does not apply.

After this is done, I will exit the app and go to Photos on my device (iPad). The stop motion scenes should be there, and able to play, just like a normal video. I never delete anything on the app yet, just in case I need to go back and change something. Although, if storage space on my device is an issue, I may find another safer way to clear space on my device.

EDITING ON IMOVIE: IPAD VERSION

After my scenes have been exported to my camera roll on my iPad, I will usually open the iMovie app on my iPad and start a new project. I open the videos tab and import each scene for my film. Sometimes, things are very long and difficult to organize, but I usually am able to sort through my scene without much trouble. First, I will make sure each scene is in order of the story. It is useful to have the script or storyboard at hand while doing this, to avoid confusion.

When everything is in the correct order, I will play the unedited film from start to finish and take note of any flaws, mistakes, or times where a scene was too long. It is useful to watch each individual shot while in production, but things will look differently when it is all put together. This editing process is just to clean things up before I get into the fun stuff.

Sometimes, there are scenes where the outside of my set, the puppets' stands, or my hands are in a frame. Usually, if this is noticed during production, I would have possibly redone the frame or shot, depending on how deep into the picture it was or how noticeable. However, a lot of times this can be fixed by cropping an entire scene or shot, just enough to cut out any mistakes. The whole shot must be cropped, or else things will look jerky. Also, make sure when cropping that your software does not change the the actual size of the screen of that shot.

CUTTING OUT A SINGLE FRAME

During my Quick General Edit in production, I try to cut out unwanted individual frames that may be blurry or reveal unwanted items. Once everything has been exported as a video, the individual frames are no longer able to be easily edited separately. If one tiny part of the video has something wrong with it, it is much more difficult to cut out.

Although the video can be paused at a particular frame, iMovie only allows a certain length of film to be cut out, and a single frame is way too short. I will temporarily put everything into the slowest slow motion as possible. Doing so will make that single frame a bit longer and able to be removed. I simply split the clips and cut out the unwanted frame. Then, I return everything back to its original speed.

RECORDING VOICES AND SOUNDS

Although I would prefer to record sounds and voices after everything is mostly edited, the recording system on my iPad sounds better than on my computer for some reason, so I will record my voice and other sound effects using my iPad. I have found that my iPad records sound much more clearly. Due to this, I record the voices and sounds right on my iPad's iMovie, using the non-fully-edited film. Although using recording equipment would be ideal, I try to stay on the lowest budget possible for now.

All the scenes should already be in perfect order and organization so that when recording, the dialogue will line up with the animation.

PREPARING THE CHARACTERS' VOICES

Back in preproduction, I talked about how I develop a character and make sure I know everything about them. I make sure they have very developed personalities. Back then, I probably would have thought of the characters' voices. That was already important as I needed to know how their voices may contribute to their actions and overall character. Now, in postproduction, I really need to make sure the voices are developed well. I talk a lot using my puppets and try to create unique voices that go well with the character. If each character has a unique voice, it is easier for the audience to identify a certain character, where the faces may not be shown.

USING OTHER PEOPLE'S VOICES

I usually do not use other people's voices in my videos or short films. Occasionally, someone in my family wants to voice a character or I want them to be a voice. I like all my voices to sound different, so sometimes asking other people is helpful. I just make sure I give clear instructions and direction, and I give the person credit in the film. If you are making your film with friends or family as a group project, you probably will want more than one person to do the voices.

USING MY REAL VOICE

I don't usually use my exact, real voice when recording as it is just the way I like to work. I may do a slight variation of my own voice, but mainly I like to exaggerate things, or I get inspiration from voices I have heard. It is just more fun that way.

CREATING VOICES

A lot of times, I will create voices that are very interesting and unique and work especially well with a character's personality. I just make sure I do not take things too far by harming my voice. If a voice is painful or difficult to create, it should not be done or you could damage your vocal cords.

ACTING WITH THE VOICE

Recording voices for characters is not just about being able to create different voices. Whether I am using my real voice or making one up, I always try to act with the voice. This means being able to give the voice personality and emotion. I try to come up with ways that the character would laugh, yell, or how he/she would create any different tones of his/her voice. You need to bring life to the character with your voice. Playing around with the puppets really helps build this skill and become more natural.

RECORDING YOUR VOICE

For recording sounds and voice, I just use my iPad. I will press the record button on iMovie and begin reading my lines as I watch the video play. I try to match everything up, which is not very difficult since the film is being played as I speak. It is important, however, to plan out which scenes I will be reading first.

Tips:

- Record one scene all at once
- Drink plenty of water throughout the process

Sometimes, I will record my entire video all at once, without stopping the record button. This helps things flow nicely, but it also can be a bit tiring and sound rushed. When there is fast paced talking, quick new voices, or character interruptions, this method can become quite challenging. Recording some voices separately is helpful. I almost always like to record an entire scene all at once to keep things flowing and natural, even if it means I must change to a different voice quickly.

WHERE DO I RECORD?

I like to go into a quiet room, such as a bedroom, that does not have any echoey sounds. It is very important that there are not any unwanted background sounds as these can easily be heard on the film if the volume is turned up enough. Sometimes, if a scene in the film is set outdoors or somewhere else that requires background sounds, I will record there, to take advantage of the natural sounds.

RECORDING SOUNDS

During the sound effect process, I will record all the sound effects needed for my short film. Again, I do not use any special equipment, just my iPad. Usually, I will watch a scene from my film and decide on what sounds will be needed.

Background Sounds: Quieter and natural sounds, such as birds chirping, people talking, etc. are sounds that help set the environment, but they are not necessarily meant to be paid attention to by the audience. For background sounds, I may record continuous sounds and then adjust the volume, to be quieter, when editing.

Louder/Obvious Sounds: Whenever the film is focused on a particular action where a sound is made, I try to make sure the sound is loud and clear enough to be heard.

Even if it is a faint sound, I try to make it obvious for the audience to notice, just like how the characters on screen noticed it.

FINDING SOUNDS

Although many editing softwares provide a library of sound effects, I like to create my own sound effects whenever I can. I will go around the house and outside, looking for the right sounds to record. It does not have to be the exact same thing producing the sound as in the film. For example, I may record the sound of dishes clinking together for the sound of glass smashing. This method works well, since I do not actually have to smash glass for the sound. Sounds can be found everywhere, from the birds chirping outside, to the scratching of a pencil.

Unlike voices, the sound effect usually do not have to be recorded perfectly to match the film. They can be recorded for a longer amount of time and then cut to fit the scene.

Sometimes, I may adjust the pitch of the sound or voice to make it sound higher or lower. I also may add in audio effects while editing, which can make the sounds more echoey, muffled, etc.

EXPORTING TO THE COMPUTER

After I have recorded the sounds, adjusted the volume, and done a general edit on iMovie on my iPad, I will export the partially edited film to my computer. Like exporting from the stop motion app, I will export using the highest quality. Then, the video will appear again in my iPad's camera roll, this time, edited. After this, I will connect my iPad to the computer and open the film into the computer's iMovie. Then, I begin working on the rest of the editing, which includes music, lighting, colour, etc.

MUSIC

Music is extremely important in a film. Just the music itself can help tell the audience what is going on.   Most films have a composer, which is a person that writes all the original music for a film. I, however, will do one of three things for my film's music:

1. Write and record my own music
2. Use non-copyright music
3. Use music from the iMovie library

I mainly will use copyright free music that I find from the internet as it gives me more variety. I also used to use the music from iMovie a lot for my videos.

ORIGINAL MUSIC

Using basic equipment can make recording your own music a bit challenging. If you or someone you know has great musical skills, you may ask them to be a part of your film.

In my short films, I mainly use my original songs when a character is singing to themselves as this does not require background music. I currently do not use original music for the entire film.

NON-COPYRIGHT MUSIC

When using other people's music in a short film or video, it is extremely important to make sure I have the rights to use it in my film, which I may enter to contests and film festivals. I will choose free music that is also non-copyright for my films. Before downloading a song, it is important to make sure the site I get the music from is an official site, and it actually owns the music. There are several sites that offer non-copyright music for free. Ask for help when browsing, selecting, and downloading music.

Film festivals are usually strict about copyright material, like music and images; they only will accept films that obtain the rights to use these things in the film. If I am using someone else's music, I make sure it is copyright free, and I have properly credited the song and composer.

SELECTING THE RIGHT MUSIC

It is important to carefully select the music for a short film. Although I do not always have a wide selection of options, I still try to find music that tells and enhances the story. The music does not have to be playing in the background throughout the entire film but during the exciting, scary, funny, and dramatic scenes, or just the scenes that need some music to help tell the story. I try to listen carefully and think about what story the music is telling. Does the music flow and follow along with the theme and story? What effect does the music have on the film? This process is really just listening, experimenting, and playing around with music to see what works best.

COPYRIGHT ISSUES

As mentioned earlier, many film festivals and contests will not accept films with copyright music or music that has been used without permission, even if the film is high quality and worthy. It is important to do things properly, making sure everything is correctly used and credited, and is not copyright. Reading things carefully, such as music rights and contest rules, will help avoid potential copyright issues. When in doubt, ask an adult to help, read things with caution, and know what you can use when it comes to not just music but also images, logos, toys, clothes, and even scrapbook papers. To be safe, I try to keep as much as I can original and non-copyright.

LIGHTING AND COLOUR

While working in the postproduction stage, I will edit and adjust the film's colour and lighting. I already mentioned back in production how I make sure the lighting is already suitable while animating, however, there still will be a few adjustments that need to be made. For this, I will use the tools included with iMovie.

LIGHTING

The lighting tells a lot about what is going on in a film; it helps set the mood of the film. If it is dark, this is telling the audience that it may be night, the scene is in a dark place, or there is something dark or mysterious happening. If the lighting is bright and sunny, it shows that this scene may be cheerful. I do not do any complex editing with the lighting. I simply will use the features on iMovie to get the look I am going for. Usually, when I edit lighting I will make some scenes darker or brighter or softer or more saturated. I try to keep things from being changed too dramatically as this can make things look too harsh or unnatural. Also, I do not try to make originally dark scenes dramatically brighter as this can make things look fuzzy and harsh.

COLOUR

Again, using the basic tools, I will adjust the colour to fit the scene in the film. I try to stick to my film's theme that I decided on back in preproduction. For example, I will remove the colour for a drained and cloudy look, often used for memories/flashbacks in a scene, or a dull moment. I may adjust the colour for a yellowish, warm tone, or more bluish for a cold, dark, or nighttime scene. I also might keep the colour looking neutral or more saturated, depending on what I am going for.

The lighting and colour go hand in hand since they both contribute to creating the film's overall look. For example, if I make the lighting darker, I may also decide to make it bluer, for a night scene.

One thing I especially pay attention to is that the lighting and colour look natural, like it could be the setting's natural lighting.

VISUAL EFFECTS

I usually decide not to use computer generated VFX (visual effects) in my film, right from the beginning of preproduction. I find it simpler and less complicated for me to make the effects physically. On a low budget, there are a few things that can be done on the computer for VFX, which can still be fun.

iMovie does not come with many "special effects", but there are a few tricks that can be done using the software.

I have not really looked into free software for effects because I find it more fun to work with physical objects and see what I can make.

GREEN/BLUE SCREEN

Although the Stop Motion Studio app currently requires a purchase to use the green screen feature, this feature can still be done using iMovie (if not Stikbot Studio).

Just as long as the stop motion was animated with a bright green or blue background, the background can be changed to any image, using the iMovie green screen/blue screen effect. There are a few risks I have found when activating the green screen or blue screen effect after everything has been animated. Since I cannot see the screen being changed as I work, things may not turn out perfectly when it is changed on the computer, later. A test can be done to make sure the green screen being used will be compatible with iMovie; also, make sure the lighting is good so that the colour is clear and bright on camera.

Here is an example of when I was using green screen with one of my stop motion videos. The background is entirely green—I used a bright green poster board for the ground and a yoga mat for the background. I placed my characters on the set and began animating them using my iPad. As I took the pictures, I was able to see the new background on the screen, so I knew it was working well. I added a Ferris wheel picture, which was taken earlier, for the background. I did this with a window behind me so that the lighting would be good. Of course, all this was done during production.

CREDITS

OPENING CREDITS

After the images are organized, I will add words for the opening credits or my studio name. I like using white or black for the words, depending on what stands out against the image. I usually will write who the film is directed by, my *studio name presents*, and the title of the film. Watching the beginning credits of movies can help with ideas for this part.

For short films, the opening credits should be kept minimal and are not even really required. Simply displaying the title of your film and the studio or director's name is enough.

CLOSING CREDITS

After a film is complete, it is important to show credits at the end. This section is a list of everyone who contributed to the film. If someone did anything to help or was part of your film, they deserve a credit. Music needs to be properly credited. Of course, if you did absolutely everything by yourself, then the credits could just be a list of your own name. When I had a YouTube channel, most of my videos were done all by myself. Sometimes a sibling would voice a character or play music for a scene, but besides that, I mostly worked alone. I still do, but I also ask others to help sometimes. In fact, I made a live action holiday short film one winter, and almost my entire family was in it, or helped out in some way. All of them were given a credit at the end.

WRITING THE CREDITS

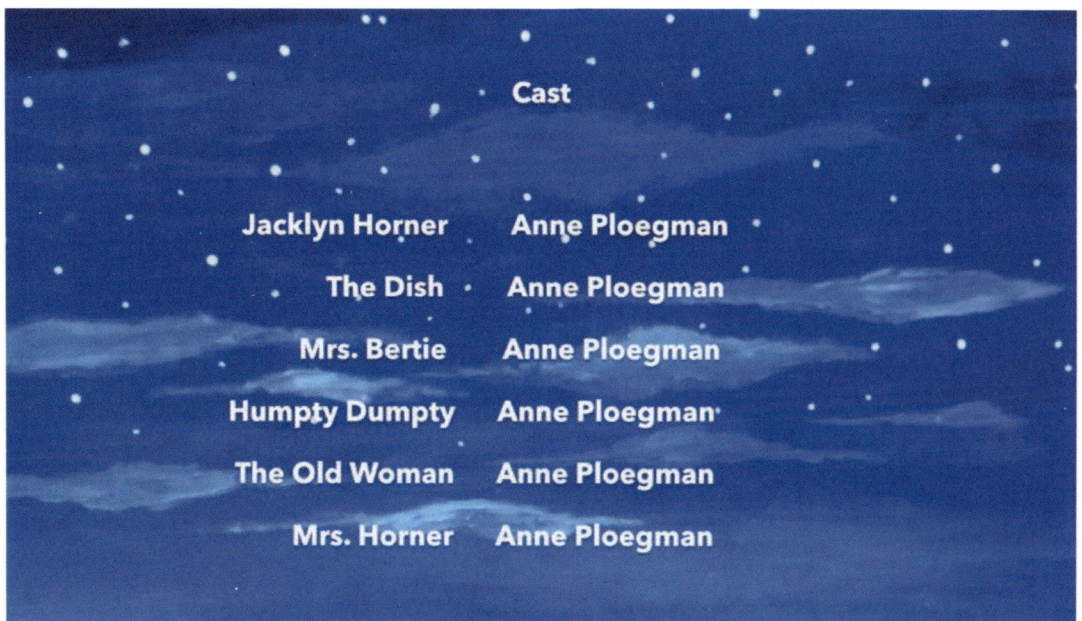

On iMovie, there is a scrolling text effect that can display words, like credits for your film. I usually will have the words displayed over a plain or painted background from a scene in my film, but this part can definitely be done more creatively. I also make sure the words are visible and stand out against the background, such as white words on a black background. Then, I will write out everyone's job and their name. Watching the ending credits of a movie can help decide how to arrange things. Also, make sure the credits are playing at a readable speed, but not too slowly. If you plan on submitting to a film festival later, note that some may require your credits to be a certain length.

FINISHING UP

Carefully examine and watch your film before deciding on officially finishing it. Even though most films will have their mistakes, the editing has to stop somewhere. I usually will know my film is complete when I have watched it several times, things move smoothly, and I am happy with it. Try to make sure there is not any jerkiness, too long scenes, or any issues that can be fixed. I always try to take out any extra, unnecessary scenes or things that are unnecessarily dragging on. Having somebody else check over the film can help spot mistakes. It mostly is important to try not to rush when finishing the film.

EXPORTING THE FILM TO A FILE

At this point, this will be the third time my film has been exported. The first time, it was exported from the stop motion app, then exported from iMovie on my iPad, and now exported from iMovie on the computer. Now, the film will become a video file on the computer, which makes it easier to store and upload to other things such as festivals or contests.

If I am planning to submit my film to a festival or contest, I should know and read the rules to make sure I am doing things correctly. Some festivals have film length and file size limits. The last time I export my film, which is when it becomes a video file, I make sure I am exporting it to the highest quality allowed for the festival I am considering entering. Many festivals also only accept a certain file format, so it is important to check that out, too. I will be talking about film festivals and contests soon.

SAVING EVERYTHING

At this point, I make sure I have not deleted anything, including all the stuff back in the stop motion app and the final stuff on the editing software. The reason is because if something ever happens, or I need to change something, I always will have the original work. If storage space is an issue however, I will export all my work onto my USB storage device and create a digital folder, just for that project. Rushing into deleting important things can cause issues when trying to change things later.

A Film by Anne Ploegman

Nursery Crimes
The Case of Humpty Dumpty

"Heartwarming and Hilarious!"

GETTING YOUR FILM OUT THERE

MAKING A MOVIE POSTER

Back in production, I talked about taking lots of extra pictures of your film. These are going to come in handy for submitting to festivals, making posters, and other things. It also is important to choose or take a photo for your movie poster. This is a poster with a main image of your film, the title, and a couple quotes by people who watched it. You can look at movie covers or posters for ideas.

Usually, the poster will be a vertical portrait, showing the main characters and setting of the film. Some posters are very simple while others are packed with all the characters together. I usually will take a picture, upload it to my computer, and do some editing. I do not do anything complicated; it is just a simple yet effective poster.

For my poster for my film *Nursery Crimes: The Case of Humpty Dumpty*, I simply set up a scene with an outdoor background—some trees, the wall, and three characters—and made the main character the focus. When I was taking this picture, I made sure there was enough room for my title to be later placed. At the bottom of the poster, I added a quote from a review one of my family members gave.

MAKING A TRAILER

A great way to promote your film is to create a movie trailer. This is a preview of your film that gives the audience an idea of what it is about. Usually, it shows several clips or parts from the film, with some sort of story introduced. Watching movie trailers is a great way to get ideas for your own.

The trailer is usually made while the editing of the film is still in progress, so it might look a little different from the actual film. Sometimes, scenes or lines are cut out, but for the most part, the trailer should be giving a general idea of the film.

Mainly, a trailer's job is to get people excited and interested in watching the movie. The trailer needs to look like something not worth missing. One important thing to remember while making a trailer is to make sure you are representing your film properly to the audience. There is nothing wrong with making the trailer seem a little bit better than the film actually is, but make sure you are showing content that is actually in the film.

FILM FESTIVALS AND CONTESTS

A film festival is a screening for filmmakers to submit to and have their film watched by a larger audience on the big screen. This is an opportunity to get your film out there, earn recognition, and possibly win awards for your hard work. If your film is selected to be screened at the festival, people get to see your film, you get to meet other filmmakers, and you may win something. The great thing about film festivals is that there are ones for all ages, including ones specifically for students.

Even if you do not attend the festival, your film usually can still win an award. Most festivals accept online submissions, which can make it easier to enter.

There are a few things to know before entering a festival:

- Many festivals require a submission fee, but many others are free to enter
- Some festivals are competitive and professionally judged
- There are different categories, age groups, and rules for different festivals
- Winning an award makes you an official "award-winning filmmaker"

Each film festival and contest has its own rules, so you will have to carefully ensure your film fits the rules. The people who work on and judge film festivals and contests receive hundreds of submissions, so be careful when making your submissions. Have an adult assist you during this process.

FINDING THE RIGHT FESTIVAL

There are many festivals out there. Some are for kids and students, and some are for professional filmmakers. Some categories have an age, film length, and content requirement. Festivals may even require your film to have been finished a certain time ago. Finding the right festival to enter can be difficult. If a festival requires a submission fee, especially a more expensive one, it is important to carefully decide if it is the right one to enter.

Filmfreeway.com is a widely used website for browsing and submitting to festivals around the world. I read about the festivals I am interested in, and I read other people's reviews and recommendations. Even if one I find is not currently open for submission, it can be entered the next year. Ask an adult to set up a FilmFreeway account for you and upload your work. Also, ask for help and permission when browsing through festivals to make sure they are safe for kids.

Reading about festival rules, awards, and even watching past award-winning films can help determine if your film is ready for the competition. It also is important to make sure the film festival you are entering is for your age group. Some festivals have a minimum and maximum age requirement, and some do not have any age restrictions at all. Knowing your competition helps determine if the festival is worth the fee. If a festival is free to enter though, there is usually nothing to lose, and possibly everything to gain, as long as you are following the rules.

I generally look for festivals specifically for students or ones that include my age. That means my film will be competing against other filmmakers my age. Sometimes, "student" can mean someone in elementary or high school, or it can mean someone in college or university. It is important to find out who the festival is for.

Another thing to note is that not all film festivals are international, meaning they may only be open to films from the same country or region as the festival's.

SUBMITTING YOUR FILM

Most festivals are accepting film submissions via FilmFreeway or directly through the festival's website. It is extremely important to read and follow all instructions while submitting.

ENTERING EARLY AND LATE

Festivals and contests have deadlines to enter your film. There sometimes is an early, regular, late, or final deadline. Entering a festival during the early submission deadline will usually have a discounted or even free submission fee. During the late submission time, the cost may be much higher. Sometimes, you will have to decide if it is worth paying the higher fee this year, or just waiting for a cheaper or free submission fee the next year.

WHAT ARE FILM FESTIVALS LOOKING FOR?

Some festivals may say exactly what they are looking for while others are open to more variety. Festivals sometimes even have particular themes. Read through festival and contest descriptions, making sure you have done what they ask of, if you want to enter. In most cases, original films that have a good story are what people want to see.

GETTING SELECTED

After you have submitted your film, you will have to wait for a while until the day when the official selections are announced. Sometimes, you get to find out within the next month, other times, it is the next year. During this wait, you can be working on other films for next year's festival, or browse for other festivals. Usually, the festival will send a letter to the filmmaker through email. After finding out if your film was selected, you will be given further instructions. The awards usually will be announced at the festival, but you sometimes do not need to attend to win an award.

NOT GETTING SELECTED

Sometimes, your film does not get selected to be screened at a film festival, and that is okay. Not everyone can get in; it is not always because your film was not good. Your film is still worthy of an audience. There are different things the judges are looking for, and sometimes the festival can only fit in a certain amount of films. Keep trying, making films, and submit to as many festivals as you can until you are selected.

WINNING AWARDS

On top of being selected to have your film screened at the festival, there also is an opportunity to win awards and prizes. Festivals may have awards for each category, or best overall film.

HAVING A SCREENING AT HOME

Even if your film has or has not been selected for any festivals, or you choose not to enter any, you can still have a screening at home. The screening is where everyone gets to see your finished film for the first time. Everyone who was involved, helped out, or just wants to support you and your stop motion movie, should be invited to watch. Try to display your film in the best way you can.

REVIEWS

After everyone has seen your film, you can ask them to write a review where they say what they liked and rate it. If you look at most movie cases or posters, you probably will see one or two reviews or quotes on the front or back. These are by critics who have seen the film and wrote something good about it. These reviews can help with promoting your film. For example, you can display people's quotes from their reviews on your movie poster.

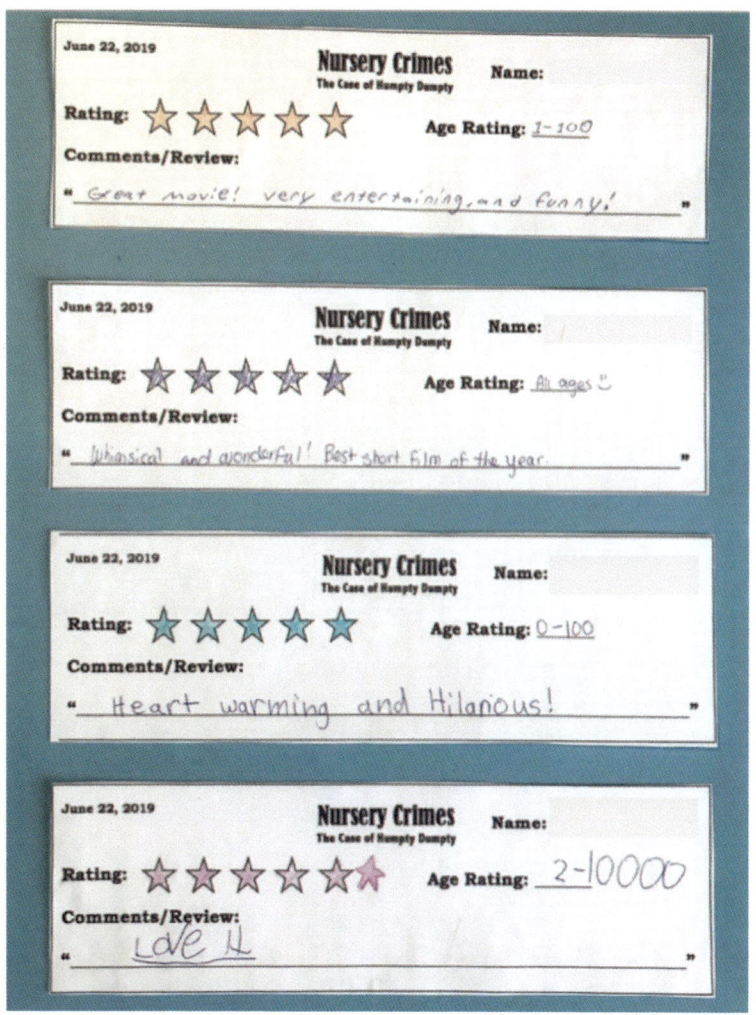

Here you can see some slips of paper I made; my family gave me reviews after they watched my film.

Make sure you continue to keep trying out new ideas, learning, and having fun with stop motion animation!

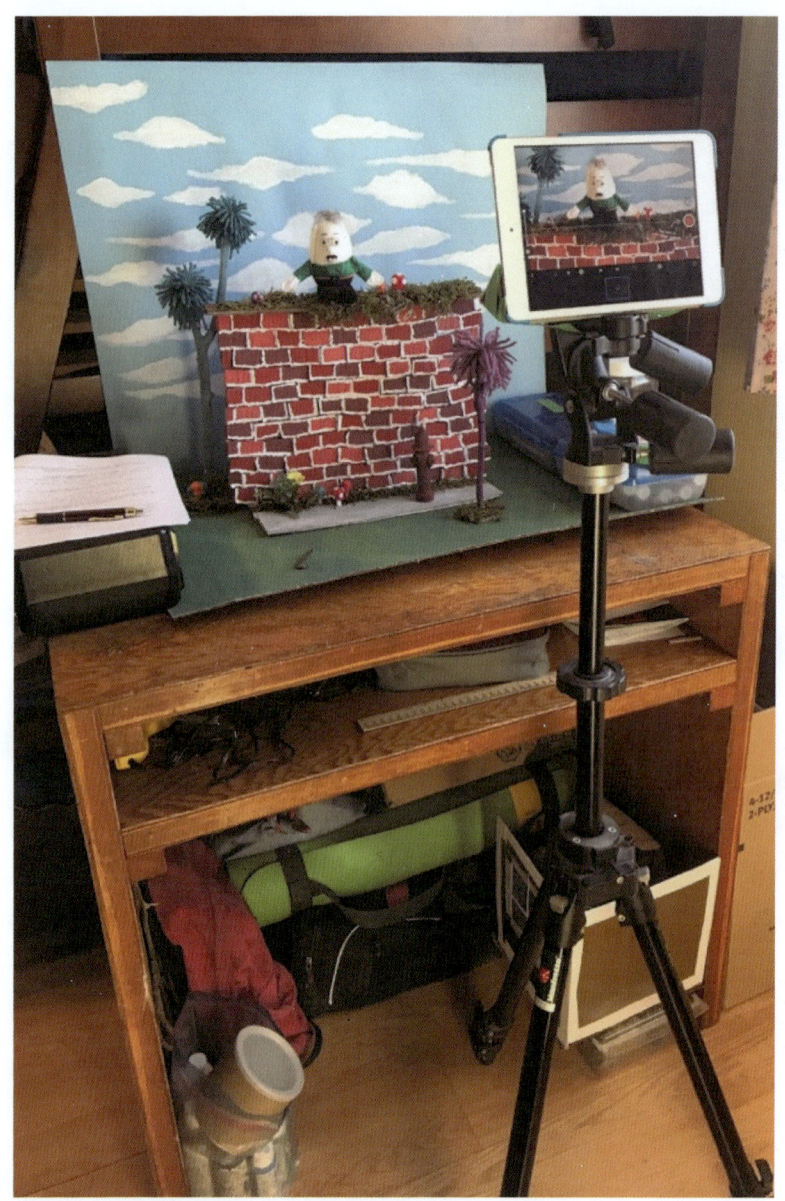

EXTRAS
MAKING A STUDIO, PRINTABLES, CLAY RECIPE, AND SUPER BASIC, QUICK SEWING GUIDE

CREATING YOUR OWN STUDIO

Making Stop Motion Films

It is convenient to have an area where you can work on your projects. I have a couple areas where I craft and animate for my films. It is important for your studio to be tidy and functional, with everything you need nearby and handy.

After finding a free area where you want to work, you can begin clearing, cleaning, and decorating your space.

My work area includes a desk for working and a shelf for storing supplies. I also used repurposed peanut butter jars and painted cocoa containers to hold items like paintbrushes, glue sticks, and craft sticks.

HOW TO MAKE PRINTABLES

Many times I will create my own designs for scrapbook papers, or other items, on the computer, to be printed and used for my props and sets. It is a great way to give your work a professional look, and it only requires the Microsoft Word (or Pages) program and a few basic computer skills.

I start by opening a new document on Microsoft Word or another writing software, such as Pages, on my computer. I then will decide what I want to create.

Let's say I decided to create a checkered floor for one of my sets. To create the design, I would simply insert a square from "shapes", then choose a colour, such as black. I also may choose to add additional details to my square, like a shiny effect. Next, I copy and paste several of those black squares, lining them up as I go along, to create a checkered design.

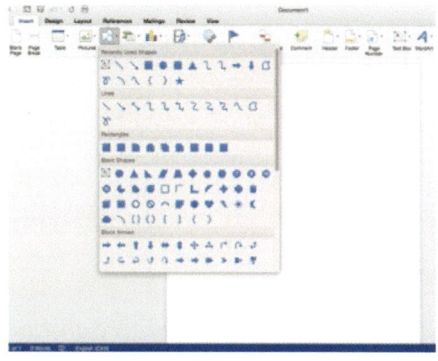
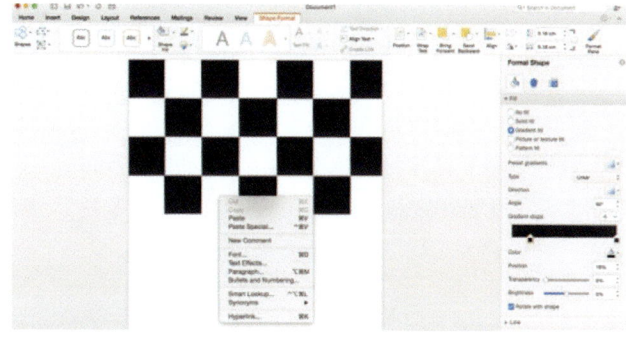

USING SHAPES AND ICONS

Almost every printable I have made has used various shapes I insert into the document, arrange, and colour. Microsoft Word provides several options for shapes, but I sometimes will create my own shapes using provided ones as pieces.

This mini airplane ticket and keyboard printables were made with the tools on Microsoft Word.

After printing the image shown, I glued it to several layers of painted paperboard to use for a miniature keyboard.

Making Stop Motion Films

GETTING THE RIGHT SIZE

At times, I will create a printable, print it out, and the image is much bigger or smaller than I expected. To prevent this, I will look at a ruler and my puppet/doll and determine the size I want the prop to be. Then, on the computer, I may adjust the length and width of the shape to fit what I want.

WORKING WITH SMALL THINGS ON THE COMPUTER

There are a few times when I am designing and creating a small prop, such as a miniature paint bottle label, and I want there to be a lot of detail, but it is difficult to work with something so small. When this happens, I will usually create what I want much larger on the computer. When finished, I take a screenshot of the image. Then, I shrink this image on the computer to the desired size, before printing.

Making printables on the computer is mostly about getting the measurements correct while working with a lot of shapes and images.

After this label for a paint bottle was made on a reasonable scale, I took a screenshot and was able to adjust the image to any size.

Creating things on the computer is a simple and convenient way to make several items and designs to be printed for props and sets. Plus, the work is original.

169

3 INGREDIENT CLAY RECIPE

Ingredients

- 1 tbsp cornstarch
- 2 tbsp baking soda
- 1 tbsp water

Directions

1. Put the cornstarch, baking soda, and water into a microwave safe bowl. Stir until it is a creamy liquid.
2. Microwave for 20 seconds.
3. Let cool. There may be a thin "crust" on the top. Stir the contents.
4. Knead until it has a smooth consistency, adding small amounts of water if it is too dry.
5. Shape it into whatever you are making and let harden overnight.
6. Store leftovers in an airtight container.

SUPER BASIC, QUICK SEWING GUIDE

Cut a piece of thread that is more than double the size of what you are sewing. Insert it into the needle.

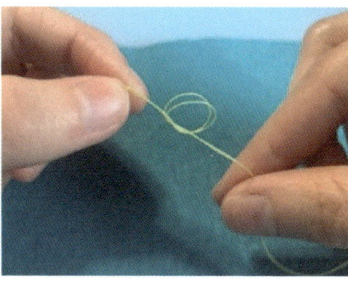

Fold the thread, joining both ends. Then, tie a couple knots at the end.

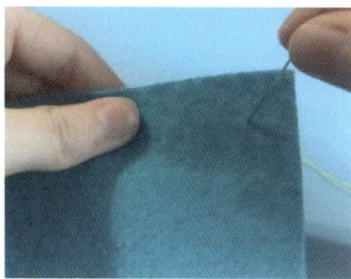

Insert the needle from the back and come through the front of the fabric.

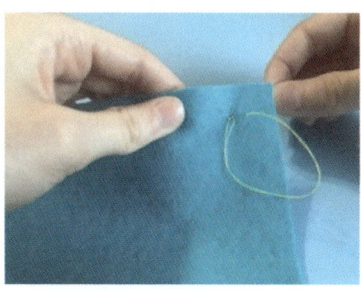

Insert the needle back to the other side of the fabric.

This is the first stitch.

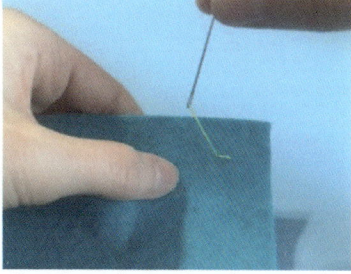

Continue bringing the needle back and forth from the front and back of the fabric.

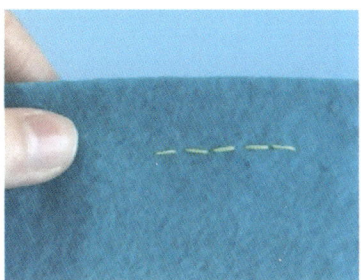

These are a few stitches.

Tie a couple knots at the back of the fabric when you are finished, and cut the thread.

When you sew two pieces together, the fabric is opened or turned right side out and a clean seam is revealed.

Bibliography

Angel, E. (2016) *Filmmaking for Photographers: The Fundamental Principles of Transitioning from Stills to Motion.* San Rafael: Rocky Nook, Inc.

Bellmont, L. and Brink, E. (2016) *Animation Lab for Kids: Fun Projects for Visual Storytelling and Making Art Move - From cartooning and flip books to claymation and stop-motion movie making.* Beverly: Quarry Books

Glassbourg, M. (2013) *Learn to Speak Film: A Guide to Creating, Promoting, and Screening Your Movies.* Toronto: Owlkids

MyFroggyStuff. (2010) *YouTube.* https://www.youtube.com/user/MyFroggyStuff/featured

Stoller, B.M. (2008) *Filmmaking for Dummies* 2nd edn. Hoboken: For Dummies, A Wiley Brand

Printed in Great Britain
by Amazon